THE EDUCATION OF THE INDIVIDUAL

The Education
of the Individual

By
ALFRED ADLER

Foreword by
CARLETON WASHBURNE

PHILOSOPHICAL LIBRARY
New York

Printed in the United States of America

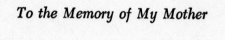

To the Memory of My Mother

credible. He is equally at home in the humanities—and in the social sciences. A letter from him while this foreword was being written came from London where he was deep in the archives of the British Museum after reading a paper at the Aristotelian International Congress in Wales. In it he says: "Once again it was painfully clear how difficult it is to communicate between natural and social scientists. I have always felt that I stand of the middle man between

FOREWORD

IN this book one has to follow unaccustomed lines of thought, leading to conclusions sometimes a bit mystifying, sometimes brilliantly illuminating. But one emerges with a fresh, widened and deepened view of a very old truth.

The book deals with "four problems an individual has to face: his relationship with others, his sense of equality, the possibility of an escape from the ephemeral, and the meaning of his actions." Man—every individual—at any given moment is an end in himself; yet any man, whether Dante or "a kid from Brooklyn," as revealed by his unconscious selection of an early memory, may be a means of seeing oneself as an end and of opening new vistas of understanding of others. In his capacity of awakening others to this deeper understanding he is the equal of any others. And a given moment in a man's life may have endless significance, may exist, not on a time line, but in eternity. Life has meaning in proportion to our ability to see and feel the significance of others and of ourselves as ends.

But this is looking at the skeleton of the book, and, like any skeleton, it indicates only the gross form, devoid of flesh and blood reality, with none of the beauty and meaning of the living thing. Who would suspect love by looking at a skeleton? And who, on reading the preceding paragraph, would guess that the ultimate conclusion of this book is that "love is a total explanation—the only thing that has offered any solution for the fate of mankind"?

Alfred Adler is a very live person—warm, deeply understanding, exceptionally modest and unassuming, amazingly erudite. He is equally at home in the humanities—and in the social sciences. A letter from him while this foreword was being written came from London where he was deep in the archives of the British Museum after reading a paper at the Arthurian International Congress in Wales. In it he says: "Once again it was painfully clear how difficult it is to communicate between humanists and social scientists. I have always felt that I am one of the middle men between the two, and I am more convinced than ever that I am."

CARLETON WASHBURNE

CONTENTS

AUTHOR'S NOTE

In 1939, a Zen Buddhist friend at the University of Chicago suggested that I write a "meditation." Maybe this is it, a verbal account in the spirit of non-verbal Zen. As for the emphasis on early memories, I owe much to the late Alfred Adler, M.D. and to Marcel Proust. Friends whose help is remembered are my brother Hans Adler, Mr. Burton Bendow, Dr. Samuel Schoenbaum, Mr. Richard Elliott, Dr. Earl S. Johnson, Dr. Carleton Washburne: *amicus certus in re incerta.* Dr. Jacques Barzun made critical comments on an earlier draft. The thought pattern began to unfold during a year spent under the auspices of the John Simon Guggenheim Foundation. My thanks to all, and to all my students!

Permission to quote specified, brief passages was granted for the following: Werner Heisenberg, *Philosophical Problems of Nuclear Science,* Pantheon Books, 1952; *Hölderlin, His Poems Translated* by Michael Hamburger, *Ibid.,* 1952; Lord Raglan, *How Came Civilization?* Methuen, 1939; Dostoyevsky, *The Brothers Karamazov,* Random House, 1950; Helen Keller, *The Story of My Life,* Copyright 1903, 1931 by Helen Keller, Doubleday and Co., Inc.; Erwin Schroedinger, *What Is Life?* Cambridge University Press, 1948. Dr. Harold Whitehall permitted me to quote his translation of a Rilke poem included in Dr. Hans Jaeger's article "Heidegger's Existential Philosophy and Modern German Literature," *Publications of the Modern Language Association of America,* LXVII (1952), p. 683.

Permission to use sources was secured as follows: R. W. Cruttwell, *Virgil's Mind at Work,* Basil Blackwell, 1946; *President Masaryk Tells His Story* Recounted by Karel Capek (transl. from the Czech), George Allen and Unwin,

1934; P. V. Sakulin, *Die Russische Literatur*, Akademische Verlagsgesellschaft Athenaion, Dr. Albert Hachfeld, 1927; Jane Ellen Harrison, *Aspects, Aorists and the Classical Tripod*, Cambridge University Press, 1919; Irwin Edman's "The Sailor and the Life of the Spirit" in *Philosopher's Holiday*, The Viking Press, 1938. I also used William Somerset Maugham's story, "The Kite" from *Creatures of Circumstance*, Doubleday and Co., 1947. My thanks for all permissions and for the efforts of Philosophical Library.

ALFRED ADLER

Brooklyn College
New York

MAN AT A GIVEN MOMENT

"Who most deeply has thought loves what is most alive."
THE individual conceived as an end, not as a means to serve ends, is a cherished concept. In a free society, the worth of the individual is the point of reference for the determination of all educational policies. But what do we mean by the statement: "The individual is an end, not a means"?

This essay is concerned with the meaning of this statement. We believe that the statement is meaningful, and that its meaning is more important to any one of us than any other meaning. But we cannot be satisfied with the assertion of a belief. We must establish and verify its meaning. For this belief is something to be achieved, not an endowment which might be taken for granted.

First of all, the unsophisticated individual is not at all sure that he is an end. It is true he is often persuaded that he ought to try his best to "amount to something," to "be somebody." But what is he before he tries so hard? What is he before he has made a success? What is he if he is not successful? With or without success, is he, and in what sense is he an end at any given moment of his life?

THE EDUCATION OF THE INDIVIDUAL

THE EDUCATION OF THE SENSES.

CHAPTER I

THE FOUR HORSEMEN

IF he is an end, what is his relationship with the world of others? Where the state is an end, the individual is a means to further the purposes of the state. An individual may be related to others by love. He may believe love to be an end. But what if he is not capable of loving, or not yet capable, or no longer capable? A successful person—whatever he calls successful—easily may consider his successes as ends, himself as a leader, the others as followers. But what is his relationship with others at such moments when there is no success? Will he suffer because of the others, or must they suffer because of him? If he "cooperates," filled with concern for others, what is there "in it" for him? On the other hand, "all out for himself," what is he to the others?

If he is an end, and so are the others, he is their equal. He is not more an end than they nor less so. But what is equality in the reality of his experience? He has heard about inequalities, economic, intellectual, cultural. He has learned to ask, "Who shall be educated?" "For what?" He is prompted to doubt whether or not, and for what, he should be educated. He has been asked to apply himself, never to delimit his aspirations, to "hitch his wagon to a star." But is he as competent as others? Is he "adequate"? Should his I.Q. be higher? (It should be higher.) His I.Q. being what it is, and other results of checking, rating and ranking being what they are at certain given moments, in what sense is he an "equal"? An "equal" in the pursuit of happiness to which he, "equally," inalienably, feels entitled?

And there is his consciousness of rapid changes. An individual's accomplishments as of a given date, here and now, may seem irrelevant tomorrow. His entire situation may have changed. The point is that the situation is expected to change constantly. A position obtained last year on the basis of qualifying tests, is not very secure. These tests perhaps are no longer valid. They should be supplemented by a CO_2 treatment, a psychological interview opening up the access to the unconscious of the candidate as he releases his inner yearnings in loquacious vapors. Experts, however, already are warning that the CO_2 treatment is not reliable, not just for any given moment.

With a bitter taste in his mouth, and with silent despair in his heart, how can the individual decide on any course of action? His actions involve other individuals. Would his actions be good if conducive to make other individuals emerge as ends, not means? Probably so. But as for him, how can he make others more conscious of their worth as ends, if he himself is not sufficiently conscious of his worth as an end? He does not trust the present moment. The present moment, says he, is no moment for action. Yet what stake had he in the past? What stake has he in the future? His fear of the future?

Confusion as to his place and function among others, doubt as to whether or not he is an "equal," the horror of the vacuities of the ephemeral, and doubt again, doubt as to the consequences of his actions,—these are the Four Horsemen.

Strangely, the Four Horsemen look alike. They are four problems with a common denominator. They are an individual's lacerations. Why? Perhaps because he has been impressed with certain tacit, undefined assumptions concerning the nature of space and time.

Consciously or not, the individual sees himself in a world of space and time as conceived by classical physics. He may never have taken a course in physics, neither classical nor otherwise, not even in high school. He nevertheless assumes that there exists an objective course of events in space and time, independent of observation. And furthermore, without using such learned terms as category and classification, he takes it for granted that space and time are categories of classification for all events, infinite space completely independent of infinite time, both independent of any observer. The individual is not necessarily a philosopher in search of the nature of reality. Yet he harbors in his mind this picture of objective reality, one and the same for all men in all places at all times.

The unsophisticated individual assumes that he is located in a static, once-and-for-all three-dimensional space. A certain area therein would be occupied by himself. The adjacent areas by the others. Any growth of the individual would necessitate a conquest of surrounding space, for his benefit, at the expense of others. To grow would mean to push and to crowd out. The very use of the German word *Lebensraum* in languages other than German, is a reminder that such visualizations of space actually occur. The history of the word testifies that they may become direly consequential in the human affairs of a *Volk ohne Raum*. A person concerned with others, the "socially minded," "responsible" individual would be made to feel like a fetus, perennially hesitant about breaking through his mother's womb. By hesitating to rob others of their living space, he would condemn himself to a low level of development. Or, less considerate, he would stretch and sprawl, distressing the unwilling mother, a threat, an enemy to mankind.

Similarly, the battle of inequality would be watched on a stage in three dimensions, yardsticks and other properties suggestive of measurement within reach. The actor, the individual, by himself in a monologue, or, with others, in dialogues, would decide or let others decide that he is too short or too tall, too big or too thin. Indeed, his intelligence and his aptitudes would turn into measurables, too short, not long enough, too thin, not big enough, to be lengthened, stretched, never stretched enough.

The sense of the ephemeral, the despair about time and changes, has something to do with the manner in which time is visualized. Time is seen as a line, starting nowhere, stretching to nowhere. The individual would mark off a certain given point on the line and call it: here and now. The entire portion up to that point would then seem irrelevant as if it were not an indication of existence and experience. Repeating the anguishing performance, again the individual would mark off a point, call it: here and now. This point again would seem like a beginning. The previous time would have become irrelevant. The past would not seem to have existed. The future would seem like a sequence of apprehended vanishing points.

There are situations where the concepts of classical physics are applicable and probably always will be. There are, however, instances well defined by physics, where such classical concepts no longer apply, i.e. the problem-situations created by nuclear physics. To cope with such instances, modern physics had to learn to shift without the conventional concepts of classical space and classical time. The hope of understanding all aspects of physics in terms of classical physics has proven an absurdity.

In psychology, the assumption still predominates that the classical concepts of space and time are applicable to the description of experiences, at least for most practical purposes. Psychological data are commonly located and dated in classical space and in classical time.

Is it possible to adopt such a procedure unreflectingly? The question must be raised. Indeed, the procedure must be challenged. The inquiry is of theoretical interest. Our motives for a challenge, however, are purely practical. We maintain that a certain aspect of human experiences cannot be explained within the conceptual framework of conventional space and time. An individual cannot be clearly seen if this uncharted aspect of his experiences is not properly focussed by the observer. "Liberated" from the dungeon of classical

space and time, the individual should be able to face his
four problems with refreshed insight: his relationship with
others at any given moment, the meaning of equality at any
such moment, the quandary whether or not such a moment
is ephemeral, the relevance of his actions at such an ephemeral moment. "Liberated," his life should not be lived as a
line of vanishing points. Could it be lived as an eternal
moment?

CHAPTER II

HE IS AS HE SELECTS AND ARRANGES

THE individual we have in mind is never quite satisfied. He always feels he ought to be different. He ought to be better. He ought to be somebody else. In short, we are thinking of the state of mind of just about all of us. Was he put into this world by a supernatural plan, miraculously, to perform a task, to pass a test? Or, not less miraculously, was he thrust into the world by accident? What does he really mean to the world? At this moment. Not after graduation. What does the world mean to him? Now. Not after he will have deserved a promotion. What is he inasmuch as he is himself? Now. What does he possess as his very own? Now. Not after a successful transaction. Does he own anything besides his loneliness in a "lonely crowd"? Perhaps the feeling of his loneliness is a priceless indication that he ever so dimly knows himself to be an individual.

If he were to tell the story of his life, what would he tell? He could not possibly tell "everything." Besides, what is "everything"? He would have to select certain bits of experiences, and, as he could not list them all at one and the same moment, he would have to arrange them, first one and then another. He would have to select and he would have to arrange. Out of the millions of bits of experiences which might be selected, he would have to select a relatively small number. Conscious or less so, the process of selecting implies the making of choices. What would make him decide on a certain selection rather than on another selection? There must be a principle underlying the process of selection and arrangement, a criterion in the light of which certain elements are deemed worth selecting, others not. Now, in our quest for the individual at a given moment in his life, we might ask: "What principle of selection determines the selection of such experiences as are fairly representative of your life?"

There is hardly an explicit answer. The question is rhetorical. The answer would have to be inferred from the very nature of a selection and arrangement. Possibly, a common denominator noticed in the selected elements could be called the principle of selection.

Frankly we do not place a very high value on an individual's deliberate, conscious efforts of selecting. Painstakingly he might start by specifying when and where he was born, who his parents were, in what town he spent the formative years of his childhood and adolescence, what schools he attended. He might then produce credentials and references, names and addresses of former teachers, ministers, employers and in-laws. He could add details concerning the service-clubs he belonged to or hoped to belong to, he could list membership in clubs implying social prestige. He might show his identification cards with photographs, and his library cards without photographs. Asked to verify his statements by referring you to the character analysis forms kept for him in the archives of his alma mater, he could have you peruse the estimates by faculty members on his Appearance, Cleanliness, Courtesy, Clear Thinking, Cooperativeness, Willingness to Participate in Campus Activities (curricular, co- or extra-curricular), Leadership. His religious views might vary as to whether or not and to what extent he thought of God as pleasant, frugal, or scolding.

Such an approach to the story of one's life is common and unsatisfactory. Documents, credentials, income brackets, social level of one's parents, one's metaphysical predilections are so many abstractions, classifications, simplifications, generalizations, standardizations and delusions imposed for the convenience of unimaginative classifiers, generalizers, standardizers, simplifiers and simpletons. Goethe knew it well: "All theory (the abstractions) my friend, is grey, but green is life's glad golden tree." Poets, novelists and playwrights are much more decisively impressed with the futility of this approach than professional psychologists and sociologists. Certain writers of realistic fiction are very much aware of the limits of abstractions. Some of them, however, like Charles Dickens, often use the chronological technique, starting with the birth of their hero and proceeding from there on, calendarwise. But a person is not a calendar. Thus, still extrinsic, taken from the calendar rather than from the person, chronology too, even in realistic fiction, is a principle of classification for the sake of lazy convenience. It divides and subdivides a person's life in calendar units.

A more sophisticated novelist was Marcel Proust. He had pungent words against the habit of labelling and classifying. Labels, he deeply felt, were never distinctive enough to render the fragrance of life's glad golden tree. Not a professional expert in human behavior, Proust created a method of recapturing his real self, and produced an achievement well worth noticing even by psychologists. The content of his writings notwithstanding, and regardless of whether or not one likes his personality, the method he used in reactivating his past experiences represents a great lesson for those who want to become individuals, ends, not means.

Our conscious, deliberate perceptions, Proust reminds us, are perpetual errors; they only allow for incomplete and often deceptive visions; they are impoverished by conscious intelligence, which eliminates from reality all that does not have any bearing on reason and action. Conscious perceptions are blurred by habit, the sluggish governor of our daily life. Our deliberate memory keeps a file of those deceptive perceptions. Yet our memory, as it relies on intelligence only, is capable of mirroring reproductions without resemblance, paled photographs in which we erroneously believe to recognize our real life.

We all have had the opportunity of appreciating these statements. By labelling the various aspects of our life with the help of abstractions, we painfully lose our selves. In a sense, we are like the powerful industrialist, Citizen Kane, who "was" so much and "did" so many things. On the point of death, however, all he remembered and seemed to care to remember was Rosebud, the young boy's sleigh named Rosebud, the shape of the sleigh, and the rosebud painted on Rosebud.

In the end, Kane's inmost aspirations were all in an involuntary memory of his boyhood. We understand. From among myriads of impressions we might remember, there are only a few which actually emerge involuntarily, without any conscious deliberate effort: a shape, a color, a sound, the peculiarly unique quality of a shape, color or sound, the shred of an occurrence ever so much more insignificant (by official standards) than many events forever forgotten. We do not know why we remember such niggardly rosebuds rather than some of the more portentous flowers of our past. To evoke our very own Rosebuds, we need not make a special effort. As far as we can tell, in remembering one little incident, rather than many other more important ones, we select certain past experiences, but we do not apply any rational, officially given standard for our selecting. Conscious or less conscious of whatever principle might underly and motivate our selection, we decide on the selection, and the selection is the result of our very own decision.

Involuntary memories often are abundantly detailed. Many of the details perhaps seem irrelevant, yet they are so pregnant with hidden meanings, more so than the weight of ponderous relevances. Little vignettes, these involuntary memories can hardly be categorized, or very imperfectly only, under headings such as "Place of Birth," "Status," "Degrees," "Adjustment." There is always more to it, so much more than what such a heading suggests. Involuntary, seemingly irrelevant by official standards of relevance, yet vivid and so gruesomely personal, these memories are one's own self, fair samplings of ourselves, representatives of ourselves as we unconsciously have decided to appoint them as our representatives. In his involuntary memories, the individual somehow is more intimately committed to himself than in other forms of living.

Alyosha Karamazov, at Ilusha's funeral, in his speech at the stone, expressed it so that they shouted "Hurrah" in ringing voices, with softened faces. May we be permitted to quote, with one proviso! Alyosha spoke not of memories only, but of good and sacred memories. He knew what he was saying. But we who do not yet know about "good" and "sacred," are quoting just for what he said about memories as such, sacred as well as profane: "You must know that there is nothing higher and stronger and more wholesome and good for life in the future than some (good) memory, especially a memory of childhood, of home. People talk to you a great deal about your education, but some (good, sacred) memory, preserved from childhood, is perhaps the best education. If a man carries many such memories with him into life, he is safe to the end of his days, and if one has only one (good) memory left in one's heart, even that may sometime be the means of saving us."

Yes, it is true that involuntary memories save a person's identity, and at the same time, offer a key to it. By comparing the content of a person's involuntary memories, a common denominator can be defined soberly and unassumingly. This denominator serves as a principle for selection and arrangement of the memory content, and whatever it is, this principle of selection can explain the person as an end, for his own sake.

The interpretations, which sometimes lead to actual misinterpretations of such common denominators, would require the considerable skill of a psychoanalyst. Depending on their orientation, the analysts would disagree. A Freudian would look for sexual commitments. An Adlerian would see compensations for real or for imagined inadequacies. A Jungian would dig up the vestiges of collective archetypes. Whatever their school of thought, analysts would use the memories as evidences for distortions in a patient's outlook, distortions which make a patient a patient, and which they hope will be corrected by psychotherapy. The therapeutic work would be operative at the moment when the patient would no longer be the way he was at the beginning of the treatment.

It is not our purpose to use the interpretations or misinterpretations of psychoanalysis.

The point to be made in this essay is that involuntary memories are human documents which can be used for the education of individuals at any given moment of their lives, and regardless of whether or not their personalities ever have been, are being, or will be improved by psychoanalytic standards.

Chapter III

HE CAN BECOME A POINTER

THE individual may be generous, open-minded, socially minded, a good "mixer," a responsible citizen, a conscientious provider, or he may also not deserve many such qualifications, or only two at best, or only one, or none at all. Deserving or not deserving, he does select and arrange such experiences as he unconsciously decides to use for the production of an involuntary memory. The product is his, inalienably. Nobody could serve as a substitute in producing the very same memory composed of the very same materials and arranged in the very same manner.

Whatever the content of his memory, it points toward issues, human and social. Thus the individual's relationship with the world consists of memories which can be used as pointers toward issues. Even a selfish monster is related to the world inasmuch as he selects and arranges experiences, each one of which is a testimony that there are issues. By offering us his pointers, he becomes our means. We can read his pointers, and then, we can trace the pointers toward the issues. Our means? What makes him an end? Clearly, the very nature of the reading material he offers makes him an end. For it is not so that certain memories point toward certain issues, while other memories point toward other issues. It may seem so on the surface. But we can never tell what we ought to know in order to understand the issues pointed out. We may be resourceful and experienced observers. We cannot be sure that we are resourceful enough, experienced enough, fully to explore the meanings pointed out by a memory. The potential meaning of a memory grows as we grow in wisdom, resourcefulness, experience and understanding. As we grow, the memory becomes a pointer toward subtler, more mature issues. The memory, then, more and more fully involves us with the world, as it offers more and more possible interpretations of the world. If it were a means only, an individual's memory would have to be a means for the reading and grasping of a definite number of issues. A memory, however, does not offer a limited number of issues. The number of issues revealed in a memory depends on the observer's resourcefulness in discovering issues. The memory (and its producer, the individual) is an end in that its meaning is like a fortress. There is no limit to the resources of human experience which might have to be mobilized to force the surrender. The individual is an end in that no definable amount of experience ever can be declared sufficient for the grasping of one single, miserable shred of one of his memories. This peculiar character of the "things" selected and arranged by an individual is not the result of his ability or his efforts. This characteristic trait of his memories makes him an individual at any given moment of his life. He is related to others and he is an end in that all the cunning of all the others might not suffice to fathom who he was at a given moment of his life. "Might not suffice"—a negative fashion of saying more positively: "Might not be wasted if spent on fathoming who he was . . .," or, triumphantly: "Might well be rewarded if devoted to fathoming who he was. . . ."

CHAPTER IV

THE CIRCUS

THERE once was a high commissioner presiding over a trial of witches. "Let me get hold of three lines of a man's handwriting!" he boasted. "I shall find a reason for hanging him." Unlike this man, but strangely invited to use a similar idea, we ask for three lines of a man's statement about himself. We shall find a reason for convincing him that the world's wisdom would not be wasted on a pursuit of the meaning of this text of three lines.

Consider the following, patently unadorned three lines, the involuntary memory of a girl, fifteen:

"When I was about three or four, I was taken to the circus by my mother's ex-boss and his wife. I recall, for some strange reason, my first reaction to seeing live clowns and wild animals."

Let us assume that this paragraph is the only contribution this girl will ever have made! Let the statement be a pointer toward issues! Are we resourceful enough to read the pointer?

The girl's experience points toward certain rather obvious issues: the relationship among members of a family; economic problems as related to family problems; recreation, excitement, enjoyment, amusement as related to the economics of life and to life within the family. There is the family, there are employment, employers, employees. The husband mentioned is not only a husband, but also an employer, the mother's former employer, the ex-boss. (Why

is an employer called "boss"? A thorny socio-psychological,
semantic issue!) The mother in the vignette points toward
issues such as attitudes towards parents, feelings of filial devotion, resentment against the routine of filial devotion, etc.
This same mother, with the connotations from within the
frame of "motherhood," also has been placed within another
frame of reference where the features of "motherhood" are
not so relevant as "market value," "dollars and cents," employers, bosses and ex-bosses. In the picture drawn by the
reminiscent girl, the "ex-boss" also has been put into an
orbit of emotions where people are husbands and wives to
each other, not only employers and employees, not only
parents and children. "Mother" selected in association with
her "ex-boss" and his "wife," thus appears not only as a
nursery mother, and not only as an appendage to a cash
register, but also, by virtue of association, as a woman who
is or was someone's "wife" (inasmuch as the reference to
the "ex-boss" husband, and his wife, reminds us that
"mother" too is to be remembered as related to a "father,"
but also to a husband).

Such are some of the obvious issues. But this is not even
scratching the surface. The girl, through her memory, points
toward the circus, the clowns, the animals, the world of
childlike excitement. She, implicitly, points toward the issue
of when and where and in what forms is there and should
there be recreation and entertainment. She points toward
the issue of whether or not a cynic should be listened to
when he says life is like a circus. Is it? Can it be? Should
it be? Should it not be? What about such forms of recreation as a visit to a circus? Is such a visit likely to restore one's
spirits? Is it a bit of unbridled primevalism? Is this a good
thing? Or should it be eradicated? How does the family fit
into the circus. The circus and parental solicitudes? What's
the relationship, if any? Love, sex, marriage, devotions—and
the circus? The circus as related to the prudent concerns of
making a living via jobs, bosses, and ex-bosses?

The girl has given us pointers. She did not realize that she was pointing. How could she have known? Her gift, the pointers, is for people only who know enough about the world to read the data of this memory as pointers toward issues. The more a person knows and learns about issues, the more significant will he find these data—as pointers toward issues. For instance, he may feel that he ought to know something about children's reactions to animals. He then might appreciate this memory in the context of a theory of the collective unconscious, preserver of totemic images of animals. This new context might direct the appreciative observer toward issues such as the role of totemic animals in primitive civilizations. A child's reactions to animals perhaps are residues of totemic beliefs. Assuming that a child's reactions to animals are derived perhaps from primitive, tribal responses to totemic images, the reader of the memory might ask for the meaning of "father," "mother," and "boss" in connection with totemic responses. We need not decide here how we feel about the theory of the collective unconscious. But we must realize that the data of a memory such as the one discussed, can become, might become, pointers toward such an issue as the theory of the collective unconscious. In fact, in a sophisticated study of this memory, the data of the memory can become pointers toward an ever indefinite number of issues.

This wretched little vignette has so much more to tell us. The issues pointed out could be studied as abstract topics, systematically, in books, monographs and articles on sociology, cultural anthropology, analytic psychology. The vignette can also be seen as a sketch done by an artist, as an artistically organic whole artfully composed of parts. As an "artist," the girl can be said to have created a harmony out of elements which, in actual life, are not in harmony, or rarely only. Would it be a waste of time to consider the girl as an artist? Interested in art, should we not devote our time to "real pictures," "real" artists, "real" art? The girl could not be considered an artist in the "real" sense. At best in a metaphorical sense. Yet in order to be able to see her at all from the point of view of artistic creativeness, we would have to draw from the resources of our experience with art and artists. In order to decide in what sense, if at all, she could be called an artist, we would have to come to terms with our own attitude toward art and artists. True, we might have learned more details about art, if we had spent our time with art "proper" rather than with the girl's memory. Paradoxically, however, it is also true that we might turn out to be more sensitive students of art after having found art everywhere, even in this girl's memory.

The girl is also a dramatist. Her memory is the summary of a dramatic plot. The setting is the circus, "Mother" and the "ex-boss" are playing parts. Dramatically, how do the two fit into this setting? Or, how are they revealed against this setting? To appreciate the possibility of their functions as "parts," we would have to be well versed in the theatre, familiar with actors, playwrights, producers, directors, critics and dramatic roles. Surely, we might learn about the theatre by taking a course in theatre-arts, and forget the girl. But we also might learn about the theatre by realizing that there is theatre even in this girl's memory concerning the circus. Nor is that all.

CHAPTER V

THE FIRST HORSEMAN

MANY more experiences are necessary for a full, exhaustive reading of the issues pointed out in this individual's single memory. This individual is an end, not a means, in that the resources of practically all other individuals would not be wasted on an effort to determine the ways in which she, the girl, points toward the world at one given moment of her life. And this can be said for any other given moment of her life, any time, even before anybody has tried to "improve" her. Any given moment of her life is significant to the extent to which there are enough observers around her, observers significant enough to provide the contexts within which her moments become significant moments. Without Mark Twain as his observer, Huck Finn hardly would be significant to anybody any time. With Mark Twain's human resourcefulness at his disposal, Huck Finn had his significant moments. For so divinely humble was Mark Twain that he made us humbly observant of Huck Finn. And all the world's resources of insight and sensitivity would not be wasted on one moment of Huck Finn's rivergodly life.

But how can an individual expect so much attention as we seem willing to grant him? It would be vain to say that he must not expect it. Growing in the light of our attention, the individual does not stifle the growth of others. His growth is not in a three-dimensional space. As his observers allot more "space" to the individual, they, the observers, "occupy" more "space" in their capacity as humanly competent observers and become assets to mankind. By devoting our energies to an appreciation of the individual's unique-

ness, we learn about the individual but also about others. To
decide in what ways he is unique, we must survey such
possibilities of performance that are different from his. One
might object that the longer we look at him, the less time is
left to look at others. This is not so. The more we notice his
uniqueness, the more intently do we have to compare him
with others. Clearly, the reference to any distinctive trait in
an individual requires a reference to other individuals. If we
notice so much as the manner in which an individual holds
his fork, such an observation implies an acquaintance with
other possible ways of holding a fork. Other people must
have been noticed holding their forks in ways distinct from
his way. In short, to notice him, we must have noticed
others.

The individual constantly refers us to other individuals.
But not because he is considerate, generous, "minding his
manners." Ever so selfish, self-indulgent and irresponsible, an
individual cannot but refer us to others. This is true even if
he is so wrapped up in himself that he cannot remember
anything else but a dish of ice-cream and how he enjoyed it.
From the millions of fragments of experiences he selects
these fragments and he arranges them, first the dish of ice
cream, then the enjoyment. The selection and arrangement
are his. Nobody else could have supplied them. The individual has decided on the selection and arrangement, and
certainly not with any concern for the welfare of others. Yet
even so, he refers us to others. The content of his memory is
meaningful only in that it means something to somebody,
meaningful within a social context of people who know how
to appreciate or how to disapprove of such drug store de-
lights as ice cream. No doubt, the individual's awareness of
his fellow men could have been expressed in more generous
terms of keener social consciousness. The point is that this
self indulgent, possibly anti-social, and surely not community
conscious person, freely selected such bits of information as
could become a pointer toward the existence of others. The

others are not remembered by him because we urged him to be considerate. He implicitly remembered them anyhow. For all we asked him to do, he might have felt perfectly at liberty to remember something with no reference whatsoever to others. He did not choose to do that. He never does. Safely we trust he never will do it. True, his choice is not proof (yet!) of his love for others. The hard fact remains: free to choose, he chose to point at others.

And he seems to matter in the awareness of others. Not (yet!) because of his devotion to them, nor because of any achievement of his, which they are bound to admire. Nor because of any prospects of any accomplishment. He matters to them—at least he might—because of his trivial revelation of himself, the selfish, thoroughly "uninteresting" memory. No efforts, no amount of resourcefulness, would suffice fully to fathom the bearings of this memory as he produced it then and there, at a given moment. Nor would all the efforts of the world be wasted on fathoming the meaning of that moment.

Chapter VI

CLEAR AND SIMPLE

THROUGH the medium of his involuntary memories, the individual teaches us that he is an end, "free," yet inevitably, ineluctably, related to society. But he hardly realizes that he teaches something so important. And he is not happy. He wants to be free, yet not isolated. He does not see how he can live in accordance with these two ideals. He probably does not discern that he actually is free, and actually is not isolated. To educate him as an individual, we would have to bring these two facts to his attention: Our persuasions will not always be successful. In many cases, however, we can succeed, with patience, genuine sympathy, and provided that we use a language so clear and so simple that our pupil will understand. The language we use must be so clear and simple that we too are able to understand what we are saying.

To make our pupil understand, we might use the following memory of a boy, thirteen:

"On my corner The city is building a library. Befor the fence was put up, my friends and I used to go into the hole which was supposed to be the cellar. It was most enjoying when the wachman chased after us and we had to make a mad dash for it."

Now "the" before "city" should be written with a small "t." It is "before," not "befor." "Enjoying" should be "enjoyable." "Wachman" is "watchman." We may bring these corrections to the boy's attention. We should. But we also must convince him that he has revealed something much more vital than his faulty spelling. Surely, the boy's performance points toward the issue of spelling. But it also points toward friends,—"pals" with whom one might have fun. Carried to a point when other people begin to resent what some call fun, horseplay is likely to invite comments. There are various possibilities for a solution. It is possible to get scared and to stop having fun. It is also possible to concentrate on one special fear only, for instance, the fear of a night watchman. It is possible that there are too many watchmen in the world, enemies of fun. This boy and his friends found out that watchmen are not necessarily "killjoys." Occasionally, a watchman even might become part of the fun. At his own expense, possibly. Is this the best of all possible courses of action? Or are there watchmen who are neither enemies, nor persons to run away from, but serious men who are guarding something valuable, so that you can take them almost seriously, not for the fun of it, but because the city has given them this job. The city? That is many persons including the parents of the boy and of his friends, taxpayers (always serious) willing to support the building of a library with many books by many authors. These books perhaps are well worth having (some of them are for certain) simply because of wonderful ideas in them, which perhaps are much fun to think about—more fun perhaps than to run away scared of a scary watchman.

Perhaps this memory argues a little too much in favor of a little too much fun at the expense of watchmen. On the other hand, this memory perhaps is a refreshing reminder for such people as are a little too easily scared of watchmen. Such scared people might end up seeing watchmen everywhere, nothing but watchmen. Their fears might incapacitate them for any kind of courage at all. Would it be a good thing for the world, the city first of all, and the readers in the would-be library of the city—to be so scared?

Such issues can be raised in a conversation with our young boy. They cannot be solved. But he can learn something about the meaning of his memory. Involuntarily produced, a commitment to his intimate self, the memory points toward many issues, many more than we have indicated. In fact, an attempt to survey "all" the issues involved, would result in a survey of "all" the world's issues. "All" inner resources of "all" people would not suffice for, yet would not be wasted on, an effort to exhaust the possibilities of this memory as it points toward human issues.

Clearly and simply—the preceding paragraph is not addressed to the boy—the boy could have mentioned other details rather than the ones he happened to select. He could have said that he did not care for a library, or that he did care because he wanted to go to college. He could have specified that it was not his idea to annoy the watchman. It was his friend's idea. Or that the pranks were his idea, but that his pals were scared; he was not. The same given moment of his life could have been exploited in thousand different ways. He decided on one way. His decision. Nobody could have made it for him. He could not give a complete list of sufficient causes why he decided on this rather than on other selections and emphases. So, where there is no complete list of causes, there is no determinism. (This again, is not said to the boy.) There is a loophole of freedom. So it was his decision, and it was his free decision freely decided upon. A decision at one given moment. A world's effort would not be wasted on it. An end, in that a world's efforts could be devoted to it.

CHAPTER VII

EQUALS: EINSTEIN AND THE MENTALLY DEFICIENT

THE first Horseman then has been eliminated. The individual is related to others even at such moments when he is most intimately committed to himself. If a shred of one of his memories may be called a detail, well, a detail offered at any given moment is worth a world's efforts of understanding. In this sense, the individual is an end, yet committed to the world of others.

It is not so easy to argue in what way the individual is an end, yet an equal to others. As an equal, he can be exchanged, replaced, and he can replace somebody else whose equal he is. How can he be an end, yet replaceable? How can he replace somebody who, too, is an end?

To understand in what way the individual is an end, yet an equal to other individuals, we must dispense with the notion that the opportunities given him are the same as those given others. Equality of opportunities is an ideal, distressingly non-existent for many. In a very real sense, nevertheless, the individual is an equal.

He offers me an opportunity. I am aware of his existence. This very awareness is my opportunity to revise my positions and to reconsider my decisions with regard to human issues of which his existence has made me aware. This opportunity he offers me may seem pertinent to me or not pertinent. Whether or not it is pertinent to me, depends not on him, but on me, on my resourcefulness and ingenuity applied in discovering the pertinence of the opportunity. I cannot say that the opportunity he offers me is less pertinent than one offered by somebody else. I can only say that I still am too obtuse to avail myself of the opportunity he offers me, and that I still am alert only to opportunities offered me by others. Nor can I say that the opportunity he offers is more pertinent than one offered by others. All I can say is that I happen to be alert enough to avail myself of the opportunity he offers me, and that I am not alert enough to avail myself of others. Whoever he is, because of the fact of his very existence, here and now or at any given moment, he offers me an opportunity for a revision of my positions with regard to human issues and a reconsideration of my decisions with regard to human issues. Issues of which he makes me aware. Neither less nor more pertinent, the opportunity he offers me is equally pertinent. In this sense, the individual is an equal.

But in what sense is he an end? An equal? Granted. Yet he can be replaced. Granted that he can become my means for the discovery of issues. So can anybody else. Inasmuch as he can be my opportunity, he becomes my means. Aware of my limitations, however, I may need him as my one and only opportunity to become aware of an issue. As a mother knows, her baby may become her one and only opportunity for joy. There are other ways of enjoying life. But perhaps not for her.

The individual offers an opportunity for an access to life. In that sense he is equal to others who, equally, might offer an opportunity for an access to life. Because of my peculiar limitations, however, this individual may be my one and only chance to become aware of a certain facet of life. The individual is an equal and an end in that he, as well as anybody else, may become the end for all my efforts of grasping life in some of its facets.

And this he may become without any special preparations. At any given moment and through the most casual, fragmentary manifestations of his self, (such as he might reveal through a shred of one of his involuntary memories), the individual, as well as any other individual, may become the end, the focal point, for all my efforts of revising and of reconsidering my positions and my decisions with regard to certain vital human issues.

Let survival be the issue. The late Albert Einstein certainly is an individual who can motivate me to ponder over the issue of survival. At any given moment of his adult life, wherever and whenever he said or did something ever so slightly connected with the theory of relativity or with nuclear physics, Einstein made one revise and reconsider the prospects of human survival. Equally, a person medically diagnosed as mentally deficient, at any given moment of his life, through one of his most casual gestures or inarticulate utterances, could become my one and only opportunity for a realization, revision and reconsideration of the problem of survival. Einstein at a moment of his Nobel prize bearing fame, not less yet not more than a mentally deficient at any inglorious moment, could become the end for all my efforts of revising and of reconsidering my positions and my decisions with regard to, say, the issue of survival.

Obviously, Albert Einstein, at a moment in his later years, just by showing his face on the television screen, would start one off. The face makes one wonder: should we or should we not sponsor the development of nuclear insights productive of much happiness but also of extermination? Should we advocate a closer supervision of nuclear researches, some legal machinery for the discontinuation of experiments the results of which might destroy us? But if we start checking up on scientists, and if we keep on checking, what becomes of the freedom of research in a free society committed to free inquiry? On the other hand, what would be the meaning of freedom with reference to such research activities as might dissolve any society, free or unfree? Should we take the position that progress must not be interfered with? Progress for the benefit of whom? Progress for a few survivors after an atomic blast, the survivors reduced to the level of cavemen and ready to start again on the road to progress? Or, should we be skeptical because of the seriousness of the threat implicit in the work of Einstein? Should we decide to be cynics with regard to the notion of progress as we learned to cherish it and as some of us now abhor it—this little Frankenstein figurine amidst the birthday cake candles for a pouch bellied, apple-cheeked Babbitt? Or should we conjure the thinning shadows of our high school Latin, quote: "Per aspera ad astra"? The dream image of the return of a Saturnian age of plenty, like Ovid's Golden Age, only bigger and better, would it be decked with atomic soda-fountains? Should we resign ourselves to becoming martyrs, martyrs of scientific progress, martyrs whose blood would cement the dancing floors for generations of cavorting divorcees?

Such queries are provocative. Certainly Einstein's least committal television nod could become my motive for all my efforts of revising and of reconsidering my positions and my decisions with regard to, say, survival.

So can the moron's, not more so, not less so—equally so.

What are we to do with him? Recommend euthanasia? Why should a hungry normal person not be given the food wasted on a moron? Shall we take the position that each human being is priceless, regardless of his condition at a given moment? That the simple-minded are closer to the mystery of the Kingdom of Heaven? Shall we say: "Where there is life, there is hope"? And ask: "Who are we to decide which case is hopeless and which is not yet hopeless?" Is the moron an outcast, a handicap, a stumbling block for a society dedicated to eugenics and to the breeding of a Superman? Or is the moron a charge entrusted to us, we being the stewards? Is he our chance to develop our humanitarian propensities, our charitableness beyond the collection plate, our sense of mercy? Or shall compassion be a sin for us as Nietzsche taught us? Or shall we, in humility of heart, endure the sight of frailty as a reminder of man's true condition? Shall we take the position of Old Spain in the days of the Counter Reformation, willingly shoulder the burden of insufficiencies so as to repent for our sinful ways in the spirit of a *memento mori?* Last not least, we also might decide to work with the feebleminded, laboriously to organize classes for retarded mental development, patiently to develop some of his crippled responses, to kindle a few flickers in almost extinguished minds so that our skills acquired in this manner, would make us more resourceful and ingenious in soliciting the proper responses from normal children.

"All truths wait in all things," Walt Whitman sang, and "The insignificant is as good as any." Indeed, the moron's most casual gesture displayed at any moment of his life, may become my opportunity—may be my one and only one, for all my efforts to revise and to reconsider my positions and my decisions with regard to the issue of, say, survival.

Survival is not the only issue which may be pointed out to me by Einstein as well as by the mentally deficient. Either one may point out an indefinite number of issues. For the purpose of simplification, however, it is easier to compare two persons with reference to one issue (defined as one). In the case of Einstein vs. the mentally deficient, we have tried to show in what sense two persons can be called equals, yet ends. So we have asserted. Now we will have to justify the assertion.

Chapter VIII

EQUALITY: VIRGIL AND A KID FROM
BROOKLYN, N. Y.

WE propose to compare a boyhood memory of Virgil, created at a certain given moment in the poet's life, with a memory produced at a certain given moment in the life of a boy, fourteen, from Brooklyn, N. Y. Deliberately far fetched and "esoteric," the issue at stake is the nature of symbolism.

It is a trite truism to repeat that Virgil is a reputed master in the use of verbal symbolism. The boy is not. Let the reader decide which one of the two offers a more pertinent motivation to face the issue at stake. And let the reader decide which one of the two might seem to offer the one and only access toward the issue, the end for all the efforts of an observer whose peculiar limitations make it necessary for him to use either one or the other for an understanding of the issue! It would be a shock, indeed, but one to be endured, if the reader should not be able to make the decision.

At a certain moment in his growth, Virgil remembered the rustic beehive huts of his boyhood in the Mantuan country. The hearths of these beehives contained perpetually burning fires whose smoke rose visibly from the hut clusters. These hut hearths had what might be called their own Vestal shrines.

So much for the memory, so much for that moment. The memory points toward many issues. It also points toward the issue of symbolism. Obviously, in order to understand we have to mobilize our equipment for the interpretation of symbolism. We might infer, for instance, that the bees mentioned here, are conceived literally as zoological specimens, interesting to an entomologist. On the other hand, the "Vestal shrines" are not literal, but metaphorical.

Later in his life, still elaborating on recollections of bee life, Virgil speaks of the beehive huts as august abodes, houses of kings, with their household gods, royal storage vaults in a kingdom of bees. In the light of such data, our resourcefulness in reading the pointers of the earlier memory is being increased. Clearly the later data are phrased in metaphors. We now feel more justified than before in considering as metaphor the "Vestal shrines" of the earlier memory. Up to this point, then, Virgil gives us the impression that his reminiscences of bees are phrased partly in a literal sense (bees being insects), partly in a metaphorical, figurative sense. Or so we are led to think.

Later still, the revered nationally renowned poet and poetic apostle of the newly constructed Augustan empire, Virgil, still weaving the memory of bee life experiences, indicates that the bees of his boyhood and bees in general are not ordinary bees only. In Virgil's epic, the *Aeneid*, Aeneas, the ancestor of the founder of Rome, is called Dardanus, the Dardanian. Virgil apparently knew that "darda" meaning bee, Dardanus was a bee-king in a mythical sense, and that the Dardanians, the king's companions, were "bees" not entomologically, not only figuratively, but ritualistically. In accordance with a Mediterranean system of royal and priestly nomenclature, the king of Lower Egypt was called "Bee." His kingdom was "Bee-land." By the same system a college of sacred men of Ephesus, the Essenes, were "King-bees." Melisseus, a legendary king of Crete, was a "Male-Bee" or Melisseus, a "Bee-man." Somehow the bee must have been a totem, that is, an animal shape used by a god or king or priest to make his appearance at certain occasions. In a ritual performance, acted out to honor the god or king, the performers called themselves "bees," and actually, literally, appeared dressed up as bees or, at least, were assumed by a religious convention, to offer this appearance. In this ritualistic sense Virgil considered the Dardanians as "bees." The mythical ancestors of Rome, then, were "bees." Indeed, the poet shows the departed spirits of the Dardanians swarming like bees in blissful abodes, awaiting their reincarnation in Italy as Aeneas' offspring. Bees, literal, yet ritualistic, swarm over the laurel tree of King Latinus. The laurels of this tree are to be reaped by the Roman people, descendants of Aeneas and of Lavinia, the latter being Latinus' daughter. The laurel tree with its bees also symbolizes the fortune of the house of Augustus. At the time when Augustus was born, a laurel tree sprang up on the Palatine Hill.

From our modern point of view, bees are "really" insects. Any symbolic use of the word "bee" has no reference to reality, but an appeal to poetic imagination. In Virgil's *Aeneid*, however, bees are *real* insects, and, at the same time, they are *real* symbols of grandeur. Naturally, nothing could be more pertinent to reality than a ritual believed to possess a lifegiving magical effect. If such a ritual required the Romans to perform as "bees," nothing was more *real* in Roman reality than these ritualistic "bees."

Through insights from the *Aeneid*, then, we have become more resourceful interpreters of Virgil's earliest memory mentioned here, about the rustic beehive huts of his Mantuan boyhood. The "Vestal shrines" in those huts no longer can be taken as a metaphor in the modern, literary sense only. These huts may now be considered as real-ecological, if you please. But these huts also may be called really mythical, mythically real, ritualistic and of lifegiving significance. And so may the "Vestal shrines" in these hut-hearts be conceived as really mythical, ritualistic realities.

Virgil's poetic purpose was not to clarify the concept of symbolism. Nor is the issue of symbolism the only one of possible interest in his earliest memory about the Mantuan bees. And, furthermore, the reader need not accept our interpretation of Virgil's bee symbolism. All we are concerned with is the illustration that the earliest (Mantuan) memory can be used for the purpose of revising and reconsidering our positions and decisions with regard to the issue of symbolism. Perhaps we had taken for granted that the symbolic meaning of a thing is not so real as the thing itself, that the "Vestal shrines" are not so real as the hut hearths. Prompted by reflections on the complexity of the problem, we then learned to read the Mantuan memory as a pointer toward the complexity of the issue. Thus, at the moment when Virgil produced the Mantuan memory, he alerted us to the possibility that the symbolic meaning of a thing may well be as real as the concrete thing itself. We need not agree that this is so. But we are stung by the Mantuan bees. They have stirred us up to the issue of symbolism.

The kid from Brooklyn too, knows how to alert us to the same issue. He does it by means of a memory which he produced at a certain moment around the time of his fourteenth birthday:

"The time I ran across Sixth Avenue behind my friend and was almost run over by a bus. I had another close call. This time a truck just missed me."

The boy remembers two incidents of danger. In either case the dangerous object was a car—first a bus, then a truck. In either case the boy barely avoided being run over. The boy must have had many experiences, not so drastic, but still worth mentioning, some pleasant, some unpleasant. He could have remembered one of those other experiences. Danger probably appeared to him in shapes other than cars, as a threatening father, as a policeman, as a nagging stern schoolteacher, as a bullying pal, as pain and disease, as the dark, as a feeling of guilt. We cannot tell. The fact remains that, from among the millions of situations, which he must have experienced, the first two spontaneously recalled, involuntarily, are the two incidents spelling danger, danger through a bus and through a truck. The bus and the truck are real, tangible, concrete objects—not symbols. Does the boy mean to say that the two vehicles of his actual past, that bus and that truck, were dangerous things? That other cars perhaps were not so dangerous? Or does he mean to imply that all cars are dangerous, cars such as, for instance, the bus that nearly hit him and the truck that just barely missed him? Does he think that things other than cars perhaps are not dangerous? Or is he governed by the fear that life as a whole is rather dangerous; life such as it appeared to him in its really dangerous aspects, in the shape of a speeding bus and of a thundering truck? Besides being real, concrete things, are the "bus" and the "truck" two symbols of life in general?

We do not know enough about the boy to answer these questions, and we are not curious. But the boy has stimulated us to ask such questions as would lead us to probe the nature of symbolism. What is a symbol? An idea represented in the form of a material thing, but not this thing itself? Or is it a thing and an idea, both in one, the thing being the idea, the idea being the thing? We do not know. But we have been stimulated to want to know. We have been shown there is an issue. Are this boy's dangerous cars faster or slower than Virgil's bees in stirring and steering us toward the issue? Until the contrary has been demonstrated, we safely insist that this boy's pointer is as usable as Virgil's pointer. Either one, equally well, might prompt an observer to revise his positions and to reconsider his decisions with regard to the nature of symbolism.

Both the bee memory and the car memory are highly personal creations, experiences selected and arranged at certain given moments in the lives of the Roman poet and of the kid from Brooklyn. The poet and the boy are equals in that either one might direct an observer toward the same issue. A classicist, the observer might be so limited as to see the issue through Virgil only. So, for the classicist, Virgil's memory might become the end for all his efforts of understanding the nature of symbolism. A social worker, the observer might be so limited as to see the issue only through the prism of, say, a dangerous neighborhood. So, for the social worker, the kid's memory might become the end for all his efforts devoted to an understanding of the nature of symbolism.

Chapter IX

EQUALITY: CLEAR AND SIMPLE

THE individual is an equal among other individuals, yet as an equal he also is an end. How are we going to teach him that this is so? We can try. But we must use very simple and clear language. He must be able to understand, and, we, his teachers, must be able to understand what we are saying.

We may tell him of a man who remembered stooping down to tie his shoe laces. Another man, we may add, remembered looking at the stars. This second person wanted to know all about the stars, and, if possible, to discover a new star. After fifteen years, both men became astronomers. Both worked together as colleagues, and, together, the two astronomers discovered a new star. That's all we know about the two men, about their achievement, and about their earlier life.

Which one of the two would seem to have prepared himself more suitably for the study of astronomy? The issue at stake is the perparation for the study of astronomy.

Obviously, the one who remembered looking at stars would seem better prepared than the one who remembered only stooping down to tie his shoe laces. The former must have been more likely to start thinking and reading about stars, at an early age, to look at pictures of stars and constellations, to go places where there was a telescope, to ask people how he might use the telescope, and what there was one should watch once it was focussed. This person also must have been quite likely to find out where one could learn more about stars so as to devote one's life to this pursuit and so as to make a living as a competent astronomer. His boyhood memory surely pointed toward an early concentrated effort of probing into this profession. Surely the other person's memory did not point equally well toward stars and astronomy.

But then again, the other man's memory did point toward stars and astronomy, not less well, not better, but equally well. Stooping down is a simple gesture but one must have learned it, otherwise one might topple over. To stoop down without falling means to know how to keep one's balance. The second man perhaps did not think so much about stars at first, but about keeping his balance. Perhaps he became quite interested in balancing as he stooped down to tie his shoe laces. The idea of balance somehow possibly made quite an impression on him. Possibly he began to notice something about the manner in which other people kept their balance, people with a special know-how such as jugglers, acrobats and dancers. Then, one day, a teacher may have noticed this second person's interest in balancing, and, perhaps, taught him something about it. Balance in the universe, in the solar system, balance between stars and planets, the sun and the moon. How could the stars stay where they were, or move where they moved, without a certain system of balance that kept them in their places or kept them moving without colliding? "Balance is a great thing," the teacher said, "balance holds the world together. Balance is not only a study for jugglers, but even for astronomers." And so the boy (the second man in the story) was so fascinated with the idea of balance in the universe that he too became an astronomer.

Which one of the two memories points toward the stars? The first one, obviously. The second one is not so obvious. Which one of the two would-be astronomers told the memory of an astronomer? The first one did. But so did the second. Neither one is less useful, neither one is more useful. Both are equally useful for the purpose (as pointers towards astronomy).

Either one of the two astronomers is equal to the other (as far as we can tell from what we know about their memories). Either one is equal to the other in this sense: Either one, at a given moment in their lives, produced a highly personal picture, a sketch, of his interests and ambitions. If nothing else were ever to be known about either one of them, either one's picture would be as good a sketch as the other's of the interests and ambitions of a would-be astronomer. They are equal insofar as neither one's picture can be convincingly demonstrated as being less valuable or more valuable for the purpose—the pointing toward the issue.

The two men are not only equals, but ends, not means. Either one of the two might be disposed in such a peculiar way that his memory is not one among others which he might have used as a pointer toward the issue. For either one of the two, his memory might well be the one and only way (the end of all his efforts) of revealing his interest in astronomy.

Similarly, either one of the two men is equal to the other, yet an end, from the standpoint of an observer. To understand either one's interest in stars, an observer might be tipped off by the first man's memory (it might be the one and only memory this observer is able to interpret as a pointer toward the issue of astronomy). But an observer might be tipped off equally well by the second man's memory (which, for this observer, might be the one and only picture he is able to interpret as a pointer toward the issue of astronomy).

CHAPTER X

THE LINE OF TIME

RELATED to others, equal to others, the individual is not satisfied. How long does his splendor last? One rare moment only, or, at most, a few rare moments? A few moments of concentration on, say, his memories, may give him confidence. But what about the vast stretches of time before and beyond these few rare moments? Graphically, time is often represented as a line leading from nowhere to nowhere. On this line of time, here and there, the individual marks off some of these moments, recalling their fragrance, oases on a desert trail. But all around the rare cases, there stretches the desert's unknown magnitude. Most of the time, there are no rare moments of concentration, there is no oasis.

Time, there's the rub. The third problem of the individual, The Third Horseman, is the ephemeral nature of his existence. In what way can he be an end? Is he not too ephemeral?

Let us be clear on one point. The individual's rare moments, the moments which really matter to him, are perhaps not charted on the line of time. Perhaps the convention to picture time as a line, graphically, must be dispensed with for a better understanding of the meaning of these rare moments.

Usually, of course, "most of the time," we are truly impressed—and depressed—by the fact that the experiences of our lives emerge and vanish in time.

Is there a time when some of us think that time is irrelevant? People are known to display such oblivious attitudes. Are they just deluding themselves? Or can we take them seriously?

CHAPTER XI

RELEVANCE IS NOT ON THE LINE OF TIME

AN experience is an event. It must be thought of as taking place at a given time. We think we can mark it off, chalk it off.

Is there anything we can do with experiences besides marking them off, chalking them off, dating them? Is there any logical justification in asking what we could do with an experience besides marking it off on the line of time?

There is a very real, logical justification. It is perfectly legitimate to take a bird's eye view of the line of time and to notice the "points" where experiences "begin" and where they "end," and the "stretches" within which they evolve. But it is also quite legitimate to look at experiences more closely, through a microscope, so to speak. Seen "through a microscope," an experience seems not to be located at a certain point on the line of time. The "microscope" does not show long stretches of time. The time it shows seems quite negligible. We might as well forget it. But it shows the experiences magnified. There is much to be seen, but no precise point of the line of time. We are speaking in metaphors, of course. We are trying to get ourselves into the mood of asking resolutely and insistently: "What is there to an experience besides its place on the line of time?"

As a word of caution, we must not confuse our experiences as we actually live them, with our psychological theories as to how our experiences come about. A really lived experience always is a rather complex phenomenon. We never really experience simple data, colors as such, sounds as such, and other experimental units which have been processed for the purposes of the psychology laboratory. A real experience, not easily defined, is something like an event, an occasion, our first day in school, a Christmas eve, a Punch and Judy show, a sleighride, a swimming lesson, a poem recited for Mother's Day, a high school prom with its never-admitted anguishes, a date, coming home from a date, and other occurrences, volitionally, and often, arbitrarily, defined as units of experiences.

Conceived in that way, experiences have the quality of being relevant. Relevant to something. To other subsequent experiences. Our feelings experienced during a Christmas eve somehow will prefigure our attitudes toward Christmas eves to come, and toward holidays and festive occasions in general. The earlier is relevant to the later. Now inasmuch as it is relevant, the experience cannot be dated, chalked off on the line of time. We never can tell at what future moments an earlier experience will become relevant to later experiences. But we know that an earlier experience is bound to become relevant at some future moment.

A Christmas eve is dated on December 24th. On December 25th, the eve is "all over," until December 24th of the following year. A Christmas eve can be dated. But the feelings, emotions and visions it aroused are relevant and must become relevant at some moment unforeseen. The relevance of these Christmas eve emotions cannot be dated.

Relevance can be conceived as an element of logic, without any material basis, or it can be conceived as a piece of neural tissue biochemically specifiable. Such conceptions will be different depending on the conceptual framework within which we attempt to define our intuitions. Relevance is something. To this one must agree. Crudely speaking of parts and wholes, we might call relevance a part of an experience. Relevance, then, is this "part" of an experience which cannot be dated. In other words, in order to appreciate the nature of relevance, we must dispense with the graphical representation of time as a line.

We never can tell at what future moments an experience

will become relevant. Yet we always reach such moments when the relevance of past experiences becomes evident. If this is so, in what sense can we say: "The experience is past"? The "past" experience is taking place whenever we experience its relevance. On the other hand, in what sense can we say: "The experience is not past, but it is taking place now (at a moment of its relevance)"? "Past" and "not yet past" are terms which seem to lose their precise meaning in the context of an appraisal of relevances.

A child has had his first piano lesson. To sweeten the tediousness of certain finger exercises, the teacher has given the pupil a little piece of chocolate. Later, no longer a child, the former piano student may become a lover of music but one of modest scope, preferring background music in a restaurant to a performance in the Metropolitan opera, and he may even have succeeded in staying away from Carnegie Hall. "I like to listen to music," he might say, "especially to background music, while I am enjoying a succulent meal in pleasant company." Reminded of his first chocolate-sweet piano lesson, this individual perhaps realizes that the earlier experience has revealed its relevance to a later situation. The date when this later situation would materialize could not have been foreseen on the day of the first piano lesson. As a historical event, this first lesson took place at a verifiable point on the line of time. As a relevance, this first lesson takes place many years later, in a restaurant with background music.

In a sense, the earlier moment (the first lesson) is not ephemeral. Something "of" (or "in" or "about") this earlier moment, its relevance, is made evident (occurs!) at a later moment (in the restaurant). One may go so far as to suggest that the later moment serves the purpose of bringing forth the fuller meaning of the earlier moment. Is, then, the later moment a means? Is the earlier moment an end?

Chapter XII

THIS ROSE IS RED

IN the foregoing chapter, experiences have been described as rather complicated events: Christmas parties, sleigh rides, piano lessons. Let us now look at one of those simpler, artificially processed experiences, expressed in the statement "This rose is red." To simplify the discussion, let it be assumed that this statement reflects an actual experience, an observation of a red rose.

In order to be able to make the statement, a person must have a reference to previous experiencs with flowers and colors. Set off against the background of many different flowers and colors, the present experience, then, is the visualization of a "rose," that is, a flower specifically distinguishable from other flowers (not roses) the person remembers, and of the color "red," that is, of a color specifically distinguishable from other colors (not red) the person remembers having seen.

Strictly speaking, the person distinguishes two elements: (1) the experience (the red rose) inasmuch as it is not yet set off against the background of memories (flowers other than roses, colors other than red). We call this element of the experience (NE), that is, experience(s) not yet set off. (2) the experience (the red rose) inasmuch as it is set off against the background of memories (flowers other than roses, colors other than red). This element of the experience we call (E), that is, experience(s) set off (awareness that, in order to say "rose," there must be lilies, sunflowers, violets, and other flowers compared with which the red shape we see is different and more like other red shapes which we remember having learned to call "roses"; awareness that, in order to say "red," there must be green, blue, yellow, and other colors compared with which the color of the red rose is different and more like the color seen on what we remember as "red roses").

There is no (NE) without (E). "Experience," "setting off," are terms used in contexts within which the Euclidean line of time is taken for granted as a principle of ordering. The very use of these terms would prompt us, therefore, to assume that (NE) comes "first," "before" (E), and that, "later," there comes (E). To make sense, such an assumption would have to be verified. The trouble is that (NE) can be assumed to exist, but its existence separate from (E) cannot be demonstrated.

We cannot chalk off a point on the line of time, calling it "The point where (NE) takes place," and then, chalk off another point, calling it "the point where (E) takes place." But this is precisely what we would have to do in order to demonstrate that (NE) comes "first" and that (E) comes "later." We do not know what (NE) is in the state of separation from (E).

We cannot say either that both (NE) and (E) take place at the same time. To verify the simultaneity of both, we have to be able to have a look first at either one (separated from the other), and then at the other. Since (NE) cannot be ascertained in a separate form from (E), this is impossible.

Even if it were possible to separate (NE) from (E) for a fraction of a second, we would be wasting our time. For, in order to demonstrate the simultaneity during the fraction of a second, we would have to find the time, concerned as we are watching (NE), to produce evidence that (E) indeed is already operative at the very instant we are absorbed in watching (NE).

(NE) is not conceivable without (E). The two cannot be conceived as a succession, one following the other. The two cannot be conceived as simultaneous either. So, since the relationship between the two cannot be visualized as successive, nor as simultaneous, the relationship between (NE) and (E) cannot be graphically represented on the line of time. Nor can one be represented without the other. Last not least, both together cannot be represented as one unit. Such a unit would have to be drawn as a line of a certain given length. The beginning of the line would indicate the point where there is (NE) only, not yet (E). A question would be: "Where does (E) start within that line?" Other questions would be: "At which point (on that line) is there more (NE) than (E)?" "At which point (on that line) is there more (E) than (NE)?" Answers are impossible. For any answers to such questions imply the applicability of the concepts of succession or simultaneity.

(NE) and (E) being two factors of an experience, no point on the line of time can be assigned to indicate whether or not (NE) takes place before or after (E) and vice versa. Consequently, (NE) and (E) cannot be located at any given point on the line of time. An experience, then, cannot be said to take place at any given point on such a line.

It might be argued that, (NE) and (E) being only two aspects of one and the same event, this event is expressed by means of two signs, (NE) and (E) being signs which are used alternately, whenever it becomes convenient to use either one, depending on the context. The event itself, one might continue to argue, is one event, not two events and, being one, it could be dated.

In order to take such a position, one would have to consider the event as the real thing, not so (NE) or (E). Real? In the physiological, biochemical sense? If there is any justification in distinguishing (NE) from (E) as "aspects" of the same event (the experience), one would have to look for physiological and biochemical elements inherent in the (NE) aspect of the event, and for another set of elements (physiological, biochemical) inherent in the (E) aspect of the event. Briefly, certain sets of neural and biochemical strata and processes would be what we would call the "reality behind" or "at the bottom of" the event. Closely linked to the strata and processes called (NE), there would be a set of strata and processes called (E). Neurally and biochemically, (E) would seem to come about as a result of material stored up at some earlier date, but not actually used up until the occurrence of (NE). Any attempt to verbalize the problem in physiological and biochemical terms would have to be phrased in some such form. Does such theory indicate the probability that experiences can be dated?

It does indicate a certain amount of probability. But there are grave objections. First of all, such a theory presupposes that psychological experiences can be and must be explained in terms of physiology and biochemistry. Granting this debatable postulate, we still have our problems, only more so.

The "material" stored up, (E), must be assumed to have been ready for participation in the making of a future experience. Until it was put together with the "material" called (NE), the "material" ready to become (E) had not been a "part" of any actual experience. At the time when (E) was stored up, nobody could tell at what moment the storage would be used for the producing of an experience. So, which date shall be given for the occurrence of the actual experience? The moment when the "material" of (NE) was "put together" with the "material" constituting (E)? The moment when the "material" constituting (E) was stored up? Assuming that there was a person who carried within him the "material" constituting (E), we would have to worry about his health, and not only because we are well disposed toward our fellowmen. What if this person dies before the moment of (NE)? Shall we say that he died taking with him the materials which could have been used for the making of an experience? Yet our late friend never lived to realize that he could have had an experience. Had he only lived until the moment of (NE)! Such are the embarrassments of a physiologist who insists that neurochemical processes are experiences, and that he can locate them on the line of time.

Disgusted, a physiologist may turn to logic, insist on a correct use of the words "now" and "not now," and say: "An experience said to take place now contains elements relevant only to 'now,' not to 'not now.'" He might add: "Memories of past events too must be considered as occurring 'now' inasmuch as they are remembered 'now.' The circumstance that such memories are made of materials stored up earlier, not now, is logically irrelevant."

Can we concede? If we do we may somewhat alleviate the irritations of a physiologist turned logician. But we still have no dates for our experiences. All we have is "now," in no way distinguishable from any "earlier" or "later," the one and only "now" of consciousness. As Erwin Schroedinger put it, this "now" is "never experienced in the plural, only in the singular. It is the immediate experience of consciousness, a singular of which the plural is unknown." There is no line of time on which experiences (in the plural) can be located. There only is the eternal "now," the eternal moment, eternal not because it can be extended on a line, but because it cannot be represented on a line.

Chapter XIII

THE MOMENT OF THE LINDEN TEA

THE purposes of our inquiry do not demand any further pursuit of the theoretical aspects of our problem. Even though experiences cannot be marked off at any given point on the line of time, we are accustomed to marking them off. We have done it, and we will continue to do it in many situations. It is not absurd, however, to treat an experience as something to which a line of time is not always necessarily applicable. In that sense, and in that sense only, it is reasonable to speak of experiences as being "beyond the realm of time," or, as Proust put it, "en dehors du temps."

This puzzling fact needs stressing. This awareness cleanses our experiences from dark connotations such as futility, and despair.

Just as the laws of Newton's mechanics are applicable for certain purposes and probably will continue to be applicable (in limited areas), so our experiences can be dated for certain purposes, and will continue to be dated. But not under all circumstances. There are situations where the laws of Newton's mechanics are not applicable. In a sense, the progress of modern physics can be described as the increased readiness to delimit the areas within which the old laws are applicable as against such areas within which they are not. Similarly, our conventional methods of ordering our experiences are effective within certain areas only. These areas have to be delimited as against what is now the No Man's Land of human experiences. Conceived as relevances or as a series of (NE)'s evaluated in the light of (E)'s, human experiences cannot be dated.

The realization that human experiences cannot be dated is not only logically defensible but also is a promise that the individual may see himself as an end. Being relevant, a given experience of his is an end inasmuch as his previous experiences may serve as means to elucidate the fuller, omnipresent relevance of that given experience.

Again involuntary memories are chosen as illustrations. Memories are relevances. They often provide the substance of (E)'s, backdrops against which to set off the yet undigested, newly added experiential contents which we called (NE)'s.

Among modern writers, perhaps the first who, unwittingly became a teacher of the "eternal" moment, was Marcel Proust. Asking how he could best begin to tell the real story of his life as it was really his own, he did not start by spelling out the date of his birthday. He looked for a spot on the surface of his life, a spot whence he might descend to the fiery center. It so happened that the spot he found was an incident from his childhood. The dipping into a cup of linden tea, of a madeleine, a piece of pastry. Other more important incidents might have come to him first. But they did not. He was not able to explain why this incident came to him first. The very fact that he did not know why this incident meant so much to him as to be remembered first, filled him with confidence. Whatever his motives for such a selection, the fact that they were not known to him, made him feel that they were genuine motives, genuinely his, unadulterated by rationalizations.

The cup of tea and the madeleine became relevant to many situations. The incident seemed intimately characteristic. In the later life of the novelist, the feeling of intimate familiarity with a situation was a feeling that this situation somehow was known to him as well as that cup of tea with the madeleine. Aunt Léonie, the whimsical hypochondriac, became intimately familiar to him, familiar like the cup of tea she had ordered to be served. Her bedroom conveyed the same sense of familiarity. So did her house, the town, the promenades from the town into the country, the promenades in the direction of the house of Swann (*du côté de chez Swann*), Swann's society of cultural parvenus. So did the longer promenade in the direction of the Guermantes, into the gardens going to seed. Intimately lived and relived, the cup of tea was a lifegiving center in the magic circle of a life.

The circle was widening. The poet grasped many new areas of experience, and deepened his feeling of intimate acquaintance with many facts of life. Yet to be intimately acquainted with something, what kind of a feeling was that? It was the feeling that one knew it well, inwardly, outwardly, as well as if it were that cup of linden tea and that madeleine dipped into the cup, in Aunt Léonie's room in the house of Combray. In that room and during that tea hour, a standard had been established, a standard for the feeling of intimate familiarity. Something became familiar to the extent to which it had the appearance of an event taking place (or having taken place) in the course of that tea hour. Finding out about the rich and the poor, about parvenus and the socially registered, about art, beauty, religion, goodness and truth, about history in general and about the history of art, music, philosophy and theology, Proust learned about all these things and, eventually, became intimately acquainted with all these things. How intimately acquainted? As intimately as if all those things had been located in Aunt Léonie's room, and as if they had come alive in the course of that tea hour in that room. That tea hour became the extra temporal, the eternal hour, the eternal moment of relevance. Its relevance occurred "whenever and wherever." That moment also became an end inasmuch as the entire world of the poet's experiences served to release the thousand facets of that jewel of a moment, the thousand and one different ways in which that moment's experience spelled its relevance.

The tea-hour situation had been made (E). Subsequent experiences, not yet elaborated, became (NE),-(E) and (NE) in a relationship uncharted on the line of time. For in what sense can one say that (E) took place in the past? The relevance of (E) took place whenever there was an (NE) to make (E) relevant. In what sense can one say that (E) took place in the present? The relevance of (E) consisted in that it provided the "historical" backdrop for any succeeding (NE).

At that moment, his life, the person (the poet), was related to the world, involuntarily, an end inasmuch as all the world's efforts at understanding would not have been wasted on trying to fathom that moment.

At that moment, the poet, the individual, was an equal among other individuals inasmuch as the tea-hour experience was an opportunity no better and no worse than any other opportunity for the revision of positions and for the reconsideration of decisions with regard to human issues.

At that moment, the poet escaped the ephemeral.

Proust taught this lesson, but he was not concerned with pedagogy. He wanted to live the moment "beyond time," *en dehors du temps,* as a poet in the holy fire of inspiration. He was right. Even in the cooler ashes of sobriety he was right. Regardless of whether or not one likes him as a person or whether or not one likes the persons he wrote about, his fanatic insistence on living the "eternal" moment makes him a great teacher of the individual as an end. Proust demonstrated more completely what all had experienced. The girl with the circus memory could try the same thing. So could the boy from Brooklyn. They could try to escape the ephemeral. Could we ourselves try to escape the ephemeral? To live the "eternal" moment? We could try. I could try it myself.

CHAPTER XIV

REDDISH NOSE IMPERIAL ROYAL

I AM now recalling my first day in school. Several details in the classroom stand out quite vividly: the blackboard, the teacher, the pale sunlight of that frosty September morning, certain faces, the desks of three little boys, a picture of Little Red Riding Hood on a wall. I notice a few things which I could not have properly described at the age of six. The classroom was located on the second floor of a ramshackle, yet dignified Imperial Royal Volksschule (Kaiserlich Königlich, not Kaiserlich and Königlich) toward the end of the long, long reign of the old whiskered Hapsburgian Apostolic Imperial Royal Majesty of Francis Joseph I, a few months before the assassination of the Archduke Franz Ferdinand in Sarajevo, a few months before the First World War. Whenever I think about the Serbs of 1914, I also think about my first class room. The more I think about the latter, the more I become aware of the former, the more inseparable both of them become.

The school was old. A new school building was in the process of being occupied, a modern one for those days, with separate cloak rooms for the children to hang up their wraps and to leave their steaming rubbers, Galoschen. Many brand new, brightly colored fairy tale pictures in clear-cut frames were hung on the white walls of the new classroom, not just one of Red Riding Hood.

I did not like the new building. The old mansion seemed more distinguished, more truly Imperial Royal, bristling decrepit like faded silk and somehow able to afford the luxury of going to seed. I still don't like new buildings with shining plumbing. I hate the monstrous apartment buildings in Greater New York. My love for the decrepit school in the Wittauer-gasse of 1913 and my dislike for the whitish new school in the Alseggerstrasse of 1913, influence my emotion whenever and wherever an old building is self-righteously torn down.

In the old building the teacher had told us about His Majesty. On the second day we learned the first stanza of the anthem about giving our Blut and Gut for our Kaiser, our Blut und Gut for our Vaterland. I liked the idea of unlimited sacrifice for the mysteriously gracious old man, His Majesty, but I did not like the line on the Vaterland, a German, not an Austrian line, not a dynastic line. (I didn't know those words, of course, but I now believe that I guessed the meaning behind them). I didn't like the bright colors of the fairy tale pictures in the new class room. The colors were gay—it was treason not to like them. But they seemed Schwarz-Rot-Gold German, not Austrian, not Viennese, not in the Spanish Viennese Hapsburgian Baroque way. (I had no such ideas, then, but I must have felt the shades). The new building was full of those crudely colored fairy tale pictures. They seemed to order you to be patriotic like a child, but in the German Wacht-am-Rhein way. I distinctly preferred the misty golden grey of the Imperial Royal way. I liked the teacher in the old building, middle-aged with a cataract in one eye (very distinguished) who used chalks of many colors (soft colors) which he applied alternately on the blackboard as he wrote carefully one word in white, one in (soft) red, one in yellow (which against the dark board was dark yellow, black yellow (schwarzgelb). Those colors I liked. His cataract in one eye was a sign of age, decrepitude, dignity, decorum, like the old bristling Knister building, and like His Majesty's slightly dripping, awesomely impressive Imperial Royal Nose Dripping (Das Nasentropferl).

Clearly, the many details in the memory are derived from

various "calendar points" of my life. Eventually, however, years ago, there must have been a moment when just about all the moods described here must have existed in me, ready to come forth as an experience. This experience, this event, the living of this memory,—when did it take place? At what moment? Whenever and wherever I was or am confronted with situations which motivate me to make a decision with regard to traditions. I question the validity of certain traditions, but I do not easily dispense with traditions. I am only too ready to discover certain spiritual values, even in traditions which, on utilitarian grounds, are said to have become obsolete. Panhandlers and other déclassés are nuisances perhaps, but to me they do not seem entirely void of a certain unaccountable dignity behind their appearance of decrepitude. The outward appearance of strength and efficiency (the bright colors of the fairy tale pictures in the new building) goads me to suspect a weakness and a frailty somewhere, cleverly or not so cleverly concealed by a huckster's wiles. Not all too cleverly. The display of failings and failures candidly admitted without self-incrimination, makes me expect that there is a fiber of sturdiness somewhere in the make up of one so gracefully inadequate. Whenever and wherever there is an issue of weakness versus strength, this earlier moment of the older school becomes relevant, influences my decision against crude muscle play in neon splendor, I, then, decide in favor of a quiet dignity whose *raison d'être* might not be palpably demonstrable. Relevant, a living relevance, this earlier moment is not in time. And it is an end in the sense that a host of new experiences only serve the purpose of setting forth the many facets of that relevance.

Quite recently, and, calendarwise, a good many years after the calendar occurrence of that first school day, I visited Quebec in Canada. There, in the city of Quebec, in the church of Notre-Dame-Des-Victoires, on the Place Royale, the enchantingly demanding 17th century market place, I noticed a marble slab referring to "Louis XIV, le grand régnant, le très illustre." The church was started in 1688. I am not particularly an admirer of Louis XIV. Nor am I particularly concerned with the victories of the French over the British in 1690 and 1711, gratefully remembered by the French colonists who considered those victories as answers to their prayers. I have no argument to offer in favor or against those who either hailed or deplored those victories. But when a sightseeing tourist commented on "backwardness" (the comment being volunteered, unsolicited), I was not convinced that the commentator, by virtue of his comment, had established himself as a sinewy pillar of "progress." I do not advocate that the house of Bourbon return to their own in Canada. But I was under the spell of the 17th century. There again occurred the living relevance of that earlier moment.

The little that has been said about that earlier moment will seem trivial enough in the opinion of some. It does not seem constructive. Let them be charitable! Let that be their opportunity to reaffirm that they are so much better—and stronger!

CHAPTER XV

TRAINING TO LIVE THE "ETERNAL" MOMENT: LANGUAGE

THE ephemeral can be escaped from, but the despair of its presence can be experienced. The recapturing of the "eternal" moment is a fundamental theme of Proust, Joyce, T. S. Eliot, Virginia Woolf, Thomas Mann. Rilke speaks of the full experience realized only in those rare moments—or is it moment?—for the sake of which we actually live:

> You only, you alone exist,
> But we waste hence until
> So much is our forwasting
> That you arise: moment,
> Sudden and beautiful,
> You arise from love, or else
> Entranced, from the effort's syncope.
> I am yours, yours, no matter how time
> May harm me. From you to you
> I am mandated. Meanwhile
> The garland hangs in jeopardy. That you may
> Upraise it up, and up, and upwards—
> Behold the festivals!

But we, the ordinary, no Heisenbergs, no poets, are timid about living our memories as "eternal" moments. We need not be timid. We too may behold the festivals. Unwittingly we are practicing the art of living the "eternal" moment. If only we knew that this practice is in the warp and woof of our daily practices!

The practice is reflected in some of our languages. He-

56 THE EDUCATION OF THE INDIVIDUAL

brew, the language of the prophets, has no tenses at all. Following Jane Ellen Harrison, we learn that the so-called Hebrew tenses do not express the time but merely the state of actions. The ancient Hebrews probably did not think of an action as past, present or future, but simply as perfective, that is, completed, or as imperfective, that is, in the course of development. The Hebrews did not express the time of an action in any verbal form. In Greek, the gnomic aorist does not indicate time. When the Homeric poet says: "A lion is glad when he lighteth upon a carcass" (*Iliad,* III, 23), he does not mean that in the past, present or future, a certain particular lion found or is finding or will find a certain particular carcass, and that that specific lion was or is or will be glad at a certain given moment. The meaning is that, at any given time, irrespective of tense, a lion, if hungry and finding, say, a stag, is glad in his lion heart. The lion, the hunger, the stag, the gladness, are in relation with each other, but out of time. In Russian, the significance of timeless aspects has been observed. To explain the Russian meaning of the motto for *Anna Karenina,* Jane Harrison had to confront the Russian version with its Greek counterpart in *Rom.* XXII, 17. The Greek phrase in turn is a quotation from the Hebrew *Deut.* XXXII, 35. In English the motto is: "Vengeance is mine, I will repay, saith the Lord." The Hebrew text, however, explains the full meaning. In Hebrew it is not said that the Lord had revenged or is revenging or will revenge but that between the idea of the Lord and that of vengeance there is an immutable, non-temporal relationship. In the Romanic and Germanic languages tenses prevail over timeless aspects, but, submerged, there still are the vestiges of the latter. For instance, in English, the adverbs modifying the forms of verbs are aspects of the action indicated by the verb, aspects irrespective of the tense of the verb which is to be modified. Summarizing her linguistic study called *Aspects, Aorists and the Classical Tripos,* Jane Harrison concludes that, "the perfective is the aorist . . . out of time," the imperfective is the duration of a line of time without indicated beginning and end. Perfective as well as imperfective, "both these aspects are primarily out of time." Truly, the venerable Diotima of humanists, Jane Harrison, left this message: under certain circumstances, time as reflected in some of the culturally prominent languages, is not a corridor leading to a judgment hall, but, like space, an inextricable labyrinth . . . an eternal, actualized present.

Chapter XVI

TRAINING TO LIVE THE "ETERNAL" MOMENT: LITERATURE

REFLECTED in languages which have been shaped by people, the experience of timelessness must be human. Some of the achievements produced by means of languages are works of literature. Great books are called timeless. In what sense are they timeless?

They are timeless in a specific, literal sense. The Homeric poems, the Bible, the *Nibelungenlied* are important memories of the human race, *Gestalten,* imaginative structures, results of selections and arrangements of impressions, thoughts and feelings. In their extant, literary forms, such works never represent a "beginning," but late phrases of long developments. Certain themes, folkloric or other, interpreted and reinterpreted in the light of experience, eventually congealed in "definitive" reactions, and are made available in critical editions. But neither do the folkloric cores ever represent a "beginning." There is no such thing as an original theme free from "later" interpretation. If the theme is (E), background material, there is no (E) isolated from (NE), new experience elaborated in the light of (E). There is (E) never without its interpretations, (NE) the gloss. From the point of view of logic, the search for an original theme is like the search for a First Cause of things, with the false belief that there is no further cause behind a First Cause. It is like the search for a Prime Mover, the Beginning of Absolute Space or Time, like Goethe's Original Plant, the *Urpflanze.* As a botanist, Goethe did not follow his intuition which informed Faust. Wagner, Faust's junior colleague (an assistant professor where Faust was full professor), a vain, complacent

Babbitt in the republic of pseudo-learning, finds that "The pleasure, by your leave, is great, to cast the mind into the spirit of the past, and scan the former notions of the wise, and see what marvelous heights we've reached at last." Faust is skeptical: "Most nobly have we, up to the starry skies! My friend, for us the alluring times of old are like a book that's sealed up sevenfold. And what you call the Spirit of the Ages is but the spirit of your learned sages, whose mirror is a pitiful affair."

Indeed the Spirit of the Ages is but the spirit of your learned sages! The interpretation of an ancient work of thought necessarily reflects the outlook of the interpreter. Surely, the latter might make a gigantic effort to "scan the former notion," to look at life as it appeared to the contemporaries of the ancient poet. The more arduous the interpreter's efforts, the more accurately will he succeed. But he will not succeed completely!

This lack of success is not caused by laziness or ignorance, or by fatigue. It is the essence of life that the interpreter cannot succeed completely. His attitude cannot be identical with that of the ancient. The reason is simple, but irrefutable. The ancient is not like the modern in that the ancient did not have to make the effort the modern has to make. Looking at Troy, a contemporary of Agamemnon did not have to make the laborious effort of seeing Troy with the eyes of one of Agamemnon's contemporaries. The latter did not have to be cautious lest he read into the picture of Troy something which belongs into the conceptual framework and outlook of the 19th or 20th century A.D. Essentially, not accidentally, and not negligibly, we receive an ancient work as an elaboration of ancient elements in the light of succeeding experience. Literally, there is an "earlier," never "alone," but always in the light of a "later." There is (E), becoming relevant again and again in new contexts, (NE). So, the reading of a great book literally, is a timeless experience.

CHAPTER XVII

NAUSICAA

IN *Odyssey VI*, we read the tale of a meeting. On the sea-shore, Odysseus, naked, a ship-wrecked stranger, meets Nausicaa, princess of the Phaeacians. The meeting was pre-ordained by Pallas Athene. She is Odysseus' patroness. She whispers to Nausicaa in a dream: "Wake up, drive to the seashore in a laundry cart drawn by mules!" The young lady and her girl companions are to do their washing on the shore. "Soon you will get married," Pallas Athene whispers, "you must get your linen beautifully clean for the wedding day, for yourself to wear, for your father and mother and brothers and for your retinue." Awakened, the princess asks her father if she may use the cart and mules. She tells him she wants to do her washing, but she is too bashful to tell him about Pallas Athene's prediction of the wedding. The father understands, smilingly gives his permission. The girls start off. The cart is unloaded; the washing completed; the clothes are hung up to dry. They have lunch, sing, dance, play a sort of volley ball. Over the entire scene there is a freshness like dawn and dew and lovely young girls. This is the moment when Odysseus appears. The girls scream, scatter in a panic—all but one. Nausicaa stands still to meet the stranger, she, a maiden so maidenlike as to be likened to Artemis, the woodland maiden goddess,—Nausicaa, a favorite also of that other maiden goddess, Pallas Athene. She listens, and, eventually, consents to show this rugged male the way toward her father's house.

Somewhere, sometime, or shall we say, once upon a time, there must have been a moment when *Odyssey VI* was cre-

ated in the form we now have. In this extant form, the canto
has a meaning which can become relevant. As a relevance,
Odyssey VI comes alive, occurs, takes place, whenever and
wherever a reader is made aware of the relevance of the
Nausicaa story to human issues.

The reader might be a folklorist interested in the folkloric theme of a hero meeting a female sea deity. Nausicaa
on her seagirt island may seem just one among other maidens
of the sea, favorably disposed toward a hero. This heroine
is humanized but otherwise comparable to Calypso, Circe,
Leucothea, other sea goddesses in the world of the *Odyssey*,
comparable also to Penelope, Odysseus' classically faithful
wife, she too a queen on a seagirt island. These feminine
images of the sea, friendly toward Odysseus in various ways,
may seem counterparts of Poseidon, the raging lord of the
sea, the enemy of Odysseus. In the background there might
be discerned the cultural conflicts between an Aegean, isle-
bound, matriarchal orientation toward Mothers of the Earth
and Sea, and a Hellenic, patriarchal influence. *Odyssey VI*
might seem relevant as a document for the existence of such
cultural conflicts (so might both the *Odyssey* and the *Iliad*
in their entirety). *Odyssey VI* might seem a restatement of
the issue: The sea a wrathful father or perhaps a loving
mother (sister, lover). The magic of the sea is felt in the
Nausicaa story, rousing, arresting, as it had exercised its
enchantments on the mind of Goethe who planned a Nausicaa poem.

Thus *Odyssey VI* might seem relevant as a document for
classifiers of folkloric themes.

But its content also might become relevant for the analysis of dreams. The dream of Nausicaa is rather typical for a
young girl preparing herself for the prospect of marriage.
The dream can be said to reflect her attempt to face realisti-
cally the less virginal aspects of married life. There will be
the presence and closeness of a husband, a brave and good
man, but one whose underwear will have to be handled by

rosy fingers. Soon, very soon, there will be married life, something to look forward to, but also something that calls for mature adjustments. Blissfully unaware of Freud, Adler and Jung, the Homeric poet associates the washing of the laundry with an impending wedding. To make it perfectly explicit, the poet insists that Nausicaa's father understood the problem, his daughter's dream hope of marriage. Asking her father for the use of cart and mules, "She was too bashful to mention the wedding. . . . But he (the father) understood. . . ." The passage becomes relevant for readers versed in the field of human development. They notice that another girl, less ready, less "mature," might have had a similar dream but with a different emphasis, possibly with feelings of fear, disgust, revolt, and unhappiness rather than cheerful hope. In Nausicaa's dream, the realistic, unromantic details of married life appear as perfectly natural concerns, natural and appropriate, even in a world of unstained maidenhood. Full of courage and confidence, the emotional climate of the dream is evidence that the dreamer faces her woman's destiny with inward assurance. At the critical moment, Nausicaa passes the test: while her companions scatter like frightened does, she stands still. She even rebukes the girls: "Come back, girls! Why this panic at the sight of a man?"

A professor of Educational Psychology might use the story as a perfect illustration in his courses. Unfortunately, the melancholy professor probably never really heard of *Odyssey VI*. So he would expand on heterosexual adjustment, the emotional development of "the" adolescent girl. He misses an opportunity. He might notice the relevance of a very much "earlier" to a very much "later" moment, and that the "earlier" becoming relevant "later," really is an "eternal" moment, not on the line of time.

With much self assurance and little power of argument, a positivist might object that *Odyssey VI* is a text he first of all actually has read, and secondly, that this text should be read from the point of view of its redactor, with no imposition of the views held after the days of Homer. In other words, the Post-homeric reader should be untouched by anything Post-homeric.

There is no such reader. At best, a reader might make an effort of freeing himself from Posthomeric ways of perceiving. Even then, the reader would not be like one of the Homeric contemporaries. Whatever they were, the contemporaries of Homer, they did not have to make a special effort of liberating themselves from such Posthomeric concerns as, say, Educational Psychology of 1958.

This truism, displeasing the positivist, is a wondrous comfort for the individual whose struggle with the ephemeral then may well be like Jacob's wrestling with the Angel: so noble an opponent cannot but enhance the status of the wrestler. Enhanced, enlivened, the individual sees Nausicaa as if she were the heroine of an individual's memory. Magnified, hallowed, projected, the result of free selection, the memory is freely ordered, pointing at human issues. All the world's efforts would not be wasted on fathoming these issues. A pointer toward issues, the memory is equal to other pointers, equal in the sense that I might need it as the one and only pointer pointing so that I am able to read the issues. It is relevant "whenever" and "wherever," and all the world's efforts at understanding would not be wasted on setting forth the thousand facets of its relevance. It is the product of a given moment, an involuntary memory of mankind. It is evidence of what can be done with such a historical moment. And it is a hint for the individual. It shows him what he could do with any given moment of his own life.

Chapter XVIII

JOSEPH IN EGYPT

THE literature of the Bible also trains us for living the "eternal" moment. We do not have in mind any specific denominational interpretation. We also appreciate the labors of critics and philologists from Richard Simon to the scholars bent on deciphering the Dead Sea Scrolls. But we intend to refer essentially to the relevance of biblical records for unsophisticated readers.

Very much alive are the biblical memories concerning young Joseph in the Egyptian prison. He was there with two fellow prisoners, both high ranking officials of the Pharaoh. The first was the Pharaoh's butler, the other his head baker. The loyalty of the two men had been subject to suspicion. They were awaiting a decision. Plagued by anxieties, their sleep invaded by nightmares, each one of the two men told young Joseph a dream. The royal butler saw grapes. He pressed the grape juice into a cup destined for the Pharaoh. He, then, presented the cup to his master who took hold of it and drank from it. "Soon Pharaoh will restore you to your office and former honorable status. All will be well with you," young Joseph interpreted. The baker saw another dream. He was walking along (apparently on his way to the palace), and on his head was a basket filled with breads and sweets. Birds flew over the basket, snatched the content. "Pharaoh will have you hanged," said Joseph. Both dreams came true.

Joseph's contemporaries no doubt considered the boy a sage, a soothsayer, supernaturally endowed. Thomas Mann, amplifying in epic splendor this telescoped account of *Gene-*

sis, discreetly accepts the old conception of Joseph as a teller
of the future. Today some among us perhaps are more hesitant in our literal use of words such as "soothsayer," "teller
of the future."

Yet even today, the dream story of *Genesis* may be found
to contain a core of literal truth for everyone. The butler's
dream is his own creation, we think. Nobody could have
made it up for him. So, in the intimate privacy of his own
dream-shaping self, the butler showed much assurance. This
feeling must have been rooted in the purity of his motives.
The office of serving as a butler to a despot required a high
degree of trustworthiness. There were occasions for such a
man to yield to the suggestions of bribery as his closeness
to his master made him a valuable participant in a plot
against the regime. A dream is a confessor as well as con-
fessing in matters of one's own conscience. Face to face with
his own conscience, in his dream, the butler was unable to
evoke any images ever so slightly suggestive of evil doing.
His heart was so pure that all he could imagine was the
honorable pursuit of his office: he had pressed the juice into
the cup and had presented the cup to his master. There was
nothing to hide. His conscience was clear. His chances that
an investigation would disclose his innocence were excellent.
And that's exactly what Joseph told him. Joseph's insight
was remarkable in that he was able to see the obvious—a
rare gift. Obviously a guilty man might lie to others, but he
would not know so easily how to lie to himself in a dream.

As for the baker, the situation was different. Obviously
there was a doubt in his mind. Would he, how would he, be
able to explain his record? He was doing his job, yes, but
was he doing a good job? In charge of providing the bakery,
he had no goods left to deliver. Could he be charged with
carelessness, negligence, and not only in matters of breads
and sweets? Who was to blame? Was he responsible for the
doings of thievish "birds"? How could he not be held responsible? Surely, he created in his dream the mood of

doubt, uncertainty, suspicion about his reliability. His chances to clear himself were poor. And that's what Joseph told him.

Again, dream analysis conceived in terms of the 20th century, a modern issue, sets forth the relevance of that "earlier" moment when Joseph explained the dreams of his two fellow inmates in the Egyptian prison. In order to establish the relevance of modern dream analysis, its power of elucidating certain past events must be demonstrated. In turn, the relevance of past events as test situations for modern theories also must be recognized. The jail term served by Joseph in Egypt has become relevant as an opportunity to test the pragmatic value of dream analysis. At what time was the Joseph story written as we now have it? This is a question which scholars might succeed in answering. They would have to use a calendar. But among other interesting elements in that story, there also is the fact that the story is relevant. As a relevance it happened and happens whenever and wherever an individual experiences its relevance.

CHAPTER XIX

TRAINING FOR THE "ETERNAL" MOMENT:
MYTHS AND RITUALS

THERE is evidence, then, that timelessness can be experienced. Vestiges of this experience are found in the structures of the most prominent languages, in the messages left by poets and in other *Gestalten* of human culture. To be sure, however, we are not dealing with an esoteric thing, but with a deeply rooted vital issue, the clear understanding of which is of a life giving effect on the individual in quandary. The issue is revealed in lives not only of the renowned but also of the humble, in the life of the girl with the circus memory, and in that of the boy from Brooklyn, even in the lives of the still less distinguished, the so-called primitives.

Indeed, the primitives are well trained in living the "eternal" moment.

Many of the so-called primitive societies have developed an intriguing relationship between myth and ritual, the former being a libretto containing the text and stage directions for the latter. The ritual has been explained as the performance which carries out the stage directions in the libretto (the myth). The performance (the ritual) is filled with magical, hallowed notions.

In the mind of the performers rituals are vital necessities, life-giving, performed to promote such vitally important events as rainfalls, the fertilization of barren soils and of the wombs of barren women, the production of abundant harvests, the birth of stalwart sons. Such rituals are performed seasonally, every year at given times. In the myths the content of these ritualistic performances are narrated as tales of events which had occurred once only. The story celebrated in the ritualistic performance is treated as one unique event, possibly a deed or feat of a mythical ancestor. The believers feel that these events happened once only, but what they call "once" takes place whenever and wherever the performance takes place. Whenever the believers perform the ritual, every single time their hero (mythical ancestor) slays the monster once-and-for-all and besprinkles the field with the monster's blood, once-and-for-all. The celebrants themselves are the hero. Each celebrant participates in the hero's nature. They slay the monster (that is, they act out the slaying of such celebrants as impersonate the monster), they besprinkle the field with whatever is meant to signify the monster's blood, each year, each year once-and-for-all. They live the life giving moment "beyond time." They do not seem to feel any disturbance at the chronometrical objection that "once" is not "whenever."

Similarly, in some fundamentalist communities of the 20th century A.D., people might tell you about the Fall of Man, a unique, historical event. Adam and Eve transgressed once, but they also transgressed and are transgressing whenever and wherever one of Adam's seed involves himself with a daughter of Eve in sin. The Fall of Man happened, happens and will happen at the "eternal" moment.

Myth and ritual can be conceived as two aspects of one experience. The latter is performed again and again. But there really is "one" performance only. As civilization grows through new inventions, these inventions have been said to serve one purpose—mainly the enhancement and embellishment of the life-giving ritual. One must come to terms with the meaning of "inventions," in order to see a connection between primitive and civilized phases of society.

CHAPTER XX

TRAINING FOR THE "ETERNAL" MOMENT: LIFE GIVING INVENTIONS

CIVILIZATION, if it is to develop, must have an atmosphere that encourages new inventions. Somewhere, somehow, somebody must have time for creative experimentation. The inventor must be relatively care-free and financially secure. A certain amount of leisure and wealth is necessary for significant, prolonged, creative experimentation.

Ancient culture provided sanctuaries for colleges of priests regardless of their religious affiliation. In these colleges, leisure and wealth were placed at the disposal of priestly groups who were responsible for cultural leadership. Even to contemplate, one must have a certain amount of leisure and wealth.

Again in the context of cultural anthropology, a main function of priests was the performance and the development of such rituals as were deemed life giving. With the advantages of leisure, priests explored new ways of enhancing and of embellishing the vital rituals, new ways of making them more vital, more effective. One example is the *Deus ex machina*. Greek drama, essentially ritualistic, created a new invention, a system of levers to catapult the impersonator of a god on the stage. The appearance of the god in this unexpected, novel manner enhanced and embellished the logos of the play.

Usually the great inventions are considered to have been brought about for utilitarian purposes, because it was found "useful" to have certain things. Lord Raglan challenged the theory that inventions were inspired by utilitarian motives.

According to Lord Raglan, the cultural achievements which turned our wandering, food gathering ancestors into settled producers were religious and ritualistic, not utilitarian. This theory seems unrealistic, but perhaps it is not. After all, corn-growing, cattle-breeding, metal working, the wheel, the sail, the loom and the brick are accomplishments which cannot be said to have been motivated through a certain inventor's insight into their necessity and usefulness. People managed for many generations without growing corn, without breeding cattle, without working metal, without wheels, sails, looms and bricks. Were their lives wasted? What they deemed necessary and useful and even life-giving were certain rituals. Rituals were useful and necessary for the preservation of life. Each one of these inventions first served the enhancement of a ritual, and, then only, eventually came to be considered "useful" in a secular sense. Devices, inventions became "useful" as people became accustomed to them for "lay" purposes other than ritualistic. Today, for instance, trains are considered (still) necessary. In 1830 they were thought a toy—a thing of leisure and luxury, embellishing idle lives. Soon, however, after people became accustomed to using trains, such vehicles began to seem necessary. Similarly, the luxury of a television set is becoming a necessity for many as so many are "getting used" to using televised information and entertainment. Let us indulge in the luxury of listening to the crotchety Lord Raglan! We soon might get accustomed to using his arguments. Once we are used to them, we even might find them a necessary equipment on our search for the individual's "eternal" moment.

"It might be supposed that inventions in connection with the ritual occur merely as part of a general condition of inventiveness, but the evidence suggests that this is not so; inventions, as a general rule, are made only by persons of education and leisure, and in most ages these could only be priests. Further than that, in most ages and countries ritual is the chief interest of the people as a whole; in the religious festivals are combined their chief pleasure and excitement in the present with hopes for prosperity in the future. The wish to embellish the ritual is the chief stimulus of invention."

In our own terms, the ritual can be called (E), a conception of life in accordance with tradition. In the course of time, new conditions emerged, new tools, new facilities, in short (NE). Yet (NE) was not made of extraneous stuff. (NE) enhanced, embellished, and confirmed the traditional conceptions of life, (E). (E) became relevant to (NE). Now relevances are not confined to given times. So (E), the ritual, confirmed by (NE), took place "again and again" and "once-and-for-all" at the "eternal" moment.

CHAPTER XXI

TRAINING FOR THE "ETERNAL" MOMENT:
THE MYTH OF THE INDIVIDUAL AND HIS RITUAL

ACCORDING to Lord Raglan, the Western World, up to the fifteenth century, learned little that had not been developed in a South-West-Asiatic ebullition of civilization at the time of the inventions of corn-growing, cattle-breeding, metal working, the wheel, the sail, the loom and the brick.

The second thrust of inventiveness occurred after 1450 and is noteworthy for such achievements as block-printing, the compass, the telescope, physiological insights (Vesalius). This second phase Lord Raglan suggests, was characterized by the separation of science and religion.

The telescope, for instance, was an "impious" invention because it enabled people to see things which "ought not" to have been there. Vesalius found within the human body organs which "ought not" to have been there either. Thus, while the first wave of inventiveness was primarily religious, the second, resulting in steam engines, Diesel motors, anaesthetics, and nuclear fissure, is then supposed to have been primarily secular.

Now was it really secular? Civilization in its second creative outburst, after 1450, the Renaissance, was to enhance and to embellish the individual. A potential Gargantua, the individual no longer was satisfied with what he could grasp with his own eyes. So he increased the power of his vision. He used the telescope. He no longer confined himself to a narrow orbit. He enlarged the sphere of his influence; he went as far as the compass needle would direct him. Like Doctor Faustus, the individual of the Renaissance "out distanced all the other Doctors, pedants, clergy and lay brothers"; hankering "after heaven's loveliest orbs," he still failed "to satisfy his restless heart." Such aspirations have been called the Renaissance Cult of the Individual. Inasmuch as he made himself the end, not a means to any religious end, the man of the Renaissance was a secular force, secularly inspired. But literally, soberly, if there was a cult of the individual, is there such a thing as a secular cult? Let's draw a lesson from primitive cultures.

For primitive man life-giving rituals and the myths, the librettoes for the rituals, are mysteries. Certain myths are really known in detail by a few of the wise old men of the tribe. They only commit their recondite knowledge to the ablest and most promising younger men, a special token of confidence in those designated by informal consensus as future leaders. One test that a boy is a future leader, is his ability to have dreams which, in their content, are strikingly similar to the myths, the content of which he has not yet been told. Surprising practice! Yet so logical, in a certain prelogical way. In those cultures, the main concerns of life were relatively simple. In a certain area, the few chances for a livelihood had to be explored. There were only a few methods, certain methods of fishing, hunting, warfare, food acquiring. Manifestly or behind a veil the myths recorded the methods used by an ideal "ancestor" in making a living then and there. An able young scion would not find it too difficult to hit upon the same few methods, to aspire toward more proficiency in the use of those methods. He even would dream about those methods, or, at least, about very similar ones. Thus the peculiar belief that individual dreams and tribal myths were assumed to be, if not identical, surely analogous, might seem quite natural. If myths are tribal memories, selections and arrangements of vital tribal experience, an individual's memories are selections and arrangements of experiences which seem vital to the individual. In a relatively simple society, both may be almost identical. Yet the individual whose dreams coincide with the hopes of the tribe, would seem a leader of promise as his aspirations are involuntarily in harmony with the aspirations of his people. Myths are religious, though, the core of primitive religious life.

We are different, but not so very much different as one might expect. We too produce memories, involuntarily, selections and arrangements of deep aspirations. Our culture, however, is complex. If there are relatively few able young tribal leaders, there surely are very, very few among us who dream in harmony with the myths of their culture. There are barely any wise old men able to tell, if they cared to, the myths of their culture. Who among us is in harmony with his culture? Who among us is able to tell whether or not somebody's "dreams" are in harmony with our culture? All we can do is to become more resourceful in establishing relevances, and to find such elements in our culture as would be relevant to our dreams, memories, and aspirations. All we can do is to make ourselves more resourceful in discovering such elements. Such a resourceful person often is called adjusted. We may call him resourceful. He certainly is "religious."

The man of the Renaissance perhaps was not despondent. Perhaps he had the courage to reach out into a world of new experiences, and to declare them relevant. This quest perhaps was his demonic determination to find relevance in an ever widened orbit of experiences and also to trust that his very own intimate self was relevant in unforeseen ways, to uncharted lands. Perhaps his *faith* was that there can and must be harmony between himself and a larger world. That the myth or dream reflected, say, in his memories, in the end was going to prove identical with a still unformulated myth of a world which had ceased to be medieval.

As for his courage, the man of the Renaissance was different from us, but only in degree. For we too might develop

a little more courage. We and the man of the Renaissance
are different from the primitives. But it is only a difference
in degree. For we too are trying to create harmony between
ourselves and the world in a deeply rooted conviction that
there is or can be or will be a harmony between our very
own personal myths and a still untold myth of the world.
So, in us too, and in the man of the Renaissance, there is and
there was religiousness, Walt Whitman's "Pervading
Religiousness."

In an analogical sense, our involuntary memories are the
myths, the stories, the logos of our lives. Our lives lived in
accordance with valuations suggested in our memories, are
the performances, the rituals. New experiences as they rush
into our lives by hours, days and years, are explored by us
and exploited as so many pretexts enabling us to produce
enhanced and embellished performances. The librettoes for
these performances, our myths, our memories, are to be
made relevant to the performances. The relevance of the
librettoes may become evident at moments which cannot
be foreseen, charted, or dated on a playbill. The librettoes
are timeless. They are precious texts, ends, not means. No
chain of new experiences (devices) would suffice to exhaust
the full relevance of those librettoes.

The primitives are religious. They know how to experience life "beyond the realm of time." The individual has
nothing to lose and everything to gain if he learns how to
experience his life "beyond the realm of time." This quest
is religious. The first explosion of our Western civilization
was religiously inspired. We may safely add that the second
phase too was religiously inspired. The first time, creative
inventiveness aimed at the enhancement, and embellishment
of communal rituals. All in all, the first thrust was effective.
The second time, creative inventiveness aimed at the enhancement and embellishment of the individual. Rituals
(lives of individuals) were to be enhanced and embellished

in harmony with directives which came from myths, the individual myths as revealed in say, involuntary memories of individuals. This second thrust, religiously inspired, was it effective? This second thrust fizzled out in the sand of the ephemeral. And it will not resume its momentum unless we learn the religious fact of life beyond time.

CHAPTER XXII

THE FOURTH HORSEMAN: THE COURSE OF ACTION

IT must not be forgotten that we do not (yet) rely on an individual's noble intentions. We are interested in him even though he has not yet made any moral improvement.

It has been assumed, however, that the individual aims at being an end, not a means. We can be sure of that, regardless of his moral attainments. We are concerned only with insights prefatory to the education of individuals, that is, persons determined (ever so confusedly) to be ends, not means. Now in order to make sure that he is an end, he necessarily must give some thought to the question: "What makes me an end, not a means?" He must compare himself with others. He must observe them. Not because he is generously disposed, but because he wants to know if he is an end, more tangibly so than others, or less tangibly so. He must have some sort of a conception as to what is involved in becoming an end, for himself as well as for others. If he were alone, he possibly would not even care whether or not he were an end.

To test the validity of his conception, he must be determined to find ways whereby the others could become ends. Eventually, he must be convinced that he, if necessary, would know how to help others so that they may become ends. This is his only chance ever of being convinced that he, if necessary, would know how to help himself so that he himself may become an end.

Ever so "selfish," the individual is interested in the possibility that he, if necessary, would be able to further other people's efforts toward becoming ends. This is a course of action in which he is bound to be interested. It is the one and only course of action in which he is, and surely better be interested.

CHAPTER XXIII

"I AM THE OTHERS AND NOTHING BUT THE OTHERS"

A MAN may look at his life, at any given moment, remember an incident, and feel that all his experiences after that incident could serve to bring forth the relevance of that incident at that moment.

But a man also may remember the content of that moment and decide that the content is a signal—a signal that there are others besides himself.

Citizen Kane, for instance, remembering Rosebud, may take the position that the most intimate thing in his life is a signal signifying the existence of people other than he, Citizen Kane. The madeleine dipped into the cup of linden tea, Proust's most genuinely intimate memory, is a signal signifying that there are individuals other than Proust. Goethe's memory of the Goethehaus in Frankfurt-am-Main, where, as a child, he threw all the crockery out of a window, a personal memory recorded in the poet's autobiography *Dichtung und Wahrheit*, is a signal that there are people other than Goethe.

In his training to help others become ends—his one and only important course of action—the individual must learn to read his most intimate memories as signals signifying that there are others besides himself.

Rosebud can be considered as an indication that there must have been a person who gave young Kane the present of Rosebud, one who made Rosebud, one who painted the rosebud, one who had taught the painter, one who sold the sleigh to the one who bought it as a present, one who defined the precinct within which the boy was allowed to cavort on Rosebud, one who objected to sleighriders outside this precinct, one who had instituted such a custom as sleighrides, one who demonstrated that sleighrides are boyish fun, one who insisted that they are dangerous, one who first drew a line between fun and danger. Many more. Throughout, the memory, this vignette reveals the existence of people other than Kane.

The madeleine and the linden tea: signals that there must have been a long line of culinary wizards able to make such pastries. The novelist's Aunt Léonie, the hypochrondriac invalid, Françoise, the wise and class conscious old maid housekeeper: signals that there must have been people holding opinions (which the aunt and the housekeeper assimilated) whether or not a child should be given such dainties, how often, under what circumstances. The visits to Aunt Léonie on Sundays, time off for rest, walks and gossips: signals that there must have been people who made a distinction between work-and-holidays, people who established the codes of propriety observed by members of families (on certain days), people who decided that one ought to go to church on Sundays, and, then, rest and take walks in contrast to people who thought that all this was not necessary.

The crockery thrown out of the Goethehaus window: a signal that there were people who made the crockery in accordance with a certain style, people who felt that you might as well smash things to pieces. Many more.

All this applies to Goethe, Proust and Citizen Kane. But it also applies to the girl in the circus, the boy from Brooklyn (Virgil's competitor), and to the fellow who uses forks, knives and spoons. Those tools are signals that there is and must have been a long line of people with views on table manners, and whether or not and in what respect Emily Post was right. The old Turkish lady who used her fingers rather than a fork, but perfectly *en grande dame jusqu'au bout des ongles:* she too is implied by one who uses a fork rather than his fingers.

Robinson Crusoe adjusting himself to life on a deserted island, alone, away from society, not only was aware that there was no society, but he desperately wished to be redeemed from his isolation. Eventually, however, he learned to shift for himslf, to rely on his own resourcefulness in many instances where, before he had been stranded, he never might have imagined that man can rely on himself alone. In this phase of self reliance, did he not prove that man can rely on himself alone? He proved nothing of the kind. To the contrary. His very condition made him more acutely aware of the existence of others. Whatever he did and felt implied that there were the others. People who gathered food, and about whose food gathering ways he must have known; people who prepared food, built shelters; people who were unhappy in loneliness; people who ardently wished to be relieved from loneliness. Clearly, Robinson Crusoe's achievement was a lesson proving not that we can do without others, but that man is not alone. Uncannily logical and consistent, Robinson Crusoe taught this lesson. In the end, on the verge of becoming "self sufficient," he found somebody.

Robinsonades often have been told to illustrate how man without "ancestors" may be assumed to begin a civilization from the beginning. Conceived in this spirit, a Robinsonade makes no sense. What men would do if they had no reference to other men, we surely do not know. The very question, however, implies a reference to many people, to a multitude of people one is not supposed to refer to.

Indeed no matter how exhaustively we explore the content of our experiences, we are unable to find anything which could not be defined as a reference to people.

But we have animal drives such as hunger, thirst, and sexual yearnings. Would we not be subject to such drives regardless of whether or not there are people? Would we not have those drives, even if we were alone? We surely do not know. To begin with, hunger, thirst and the sexual drive have to be defined. Words have to be used, references to a long line of people who developed such languages as have been put down in dictionaries. Implicitly, speaking of animal drives, we also point toward people who, somewhere, at some time, must have distinguished (and taught others to distinguish) between animal drives as against aspirations deemed more specifically human and humane. We point toward all those who, somewhere, at some time, affixed moral, religious meanings to our attitudes with regard to the physical and spiritual. And as for our question: "What would we do, alone, given only to the satisfaction of primitive wants?," we are pointing toward all the people who, then, happen not to be there, even though they might have been there, and who happen not to incommode us with such concerns as might incommode us.

So, the individual who wants to be an end, is assumed here to be interested in testing his ability to help others emerge as ends. The task requires training. He gets a good start, though, if he consistently reads his experiences as signals signifying that there are people. The individual, the would-be end, is bound to conclude that his most intimate experiences can become means pointing toward ends. The ends are the people.

CHAPTER XXIV

ACTION, GOOD OR BAD

WE have come to the conclusion that it is very much the concern of the individual to help others become ends. For this is the only way he can assure himself that he knows something about the process of becoming an end. The more people he is able to help toward this goal the more convinced he can be that he himself can achieve it. If he cannot help people, if he can help very few people only, faith in his abilities will be shaken.

Within the framework of this reasoning, the actions of an individual will seem "good" or "better" as they are signals happily pointing toward a large and larger number of people. Likewise, his actions will seem "bad" or "worse" as they are signals pointing toward a relatively smaller number of people. Apparently we are "good" or "better" as our actions imply the gladly accepted awareness of many and more people who simply cannot be ignored. Similarly we are "bad" or "worse" as our actions imply an awareness of fewer people than could (should) be noticed.

A teacher, for instance, may be qualified as "good" if his approach to a pupil indicates his awareness of the effect of this child on other children in the room. This teacher may be said to be "better" if his approach indicates his awareness of the effect of this child on the entire school, the town, the world.

On the other hand, a thief is "bad" inasmuch as his enterprises prompt him to hope that relatively few people will know what he is doing. Preferably, no one would know except his accomplices and only when he could not dispense with their services. The life of a thief is such that he is fortunate if few are aware of his existence.

The criterion seems valid with regard to minute courses of action. Is it "good" or "bad" to know something about punctuation? To put a comma where it belongs is not much of an action, but is an action just the same. It is "well" done if it implies the awareness of many people who might benefit from an effective system of written communication. In other words, the action is "good" if it implies that we have a rather high regard for many people, a regard so high, indeed, that we really wish to avoid equivocation when we write them. So we put the commas where they belong. A teacher, however, might tyrannize his class, drilling the use of commas so that commas turn into nightmares for the less skillful children. Such a martinet's action is "bad" inasmuch as he gladly accepts only the very few who master the commas, trying to create a world in which one should be aware of such people only as know about commas. A decision as to how "good" or "bad" it is to insist on proper punctuation, depends on whether or not such insistence adds to, or detracts from the glad acceptance of more people.

There are courses of action much loftier than the insistence on punctuation. Loftier, yes. Inasmuch as such courses of action are much more clearly indicative of a glad awareness of more people.

We will have to concern ourselves with such loftier courses of action. In the meantime, let it be made clear that an individual, aware of the existence of many people, need not be noble or magnanimous. He gladly realizes that his experiences may serve as means toward ends, as pointers toward people, the pointers being the means, the people being the ends. For the time being his gladness need not be generosity. He simply is glad to realize how easy it is to help people become ends. All he has got to do is to conceive his experiences as pointers (means) toward ends (people). Naturally he would be glad that this is so easy. For if this service is so easily rendered, others should find it easy to render it even to him. He himself might do it for himself.

CHAPTER XXV

ACTION, "WORSE" OR "BETTER"

THERE is a young Mexican boy in John Steinbeck's novel *The Forgotten Village.* He lives in the Mexican desert. The villagers subsist on what a reader might call a low level of civilization, dominated by superstitions. There have been cases of typhoid fever. Several children are taken ill. A medicine woman advises applying the dried skin of a snake on the little patients' bellies. This is done. Some of the children get well. But there still are casualties. The young boy loses faith in the effectiveness of the snakeskin charm. His friend, the school teacher in that village, persuades him that such charms are no sound therapy because typhoid fever is caused by a virus. The infected wells, the school teacher tells him, must be disinfected. The patients must be given shots, all the folks, old and young, must get shots too, prophylactic. So the boy and the schoolteacher secretly drive to the city. There is a modern hospital with doctors, nurses, and a good deal of necessary appliances and equipment. Accompanied by a doctor, a nurse, and with the suitable materials, the two progressive villagers drive up to the village. The wells are disinfected, shots are administered to as many children as are allowed by their parents.

The trouble is that not everybody is willing to be inoculated. The medicine woman is very much against the whole program. The doctor and nurse are asked to leave. The boy himself is disowned by his father. He leaves the forgotten village for the kind of society that the school teacher, the doctor, the nurse and the city have introduced him to.

Our first impression, quite naturally, is that the boy was

right. His course of action was "good," "better" than the one taken by the superstitious parents and the medicine woman.

But it is not so easy to explain what we mean. In what sense was the boy "better" advised than the villagers? In what sense was their action "worse"? We are firm in our conviction that experience has taught us to rely on a doctor's methods rather than on the practices of a medicine woman. The boy, however, had no experience with modern medical practices. He happened to have faith in the teacher's opinions. The teacher, however, had no statistical evidence that medical treatment of typhoid fever yields results in more cases than the laying on of a snake skin. He too happened to have faith, faith in the doctors of great cities. The old fashioned villagers had no way of comparing the snake skin results with doctors' treatments. They happened to have faith in the ways of the medicine woman. She too happened to have faith, faith in the methods transmitted to her from times immemorial.

For the villagers the old method was "good." If a child got well, the snake skin must have done the trick. Good! If a child died, there must have been a mistake. Somehow the snake skin ritual had not been accurately performed. Properly applied, the snake skin would have helped. This conviction was good! Furthermore, a departed child became an angel. To Heaven he went, on his little head a brand new sombrero. This too was good! In the forgotten village, within a sphere of undisturbed beliefs, usages and convictions, the snake skin method was "good" under all circumstances. To operate in accordance with this method was "good" inasmuch as this action implied the acceptance of all the people involved: the people who hoped to recover as a result of the correct performance of the ritual, the people who expected and accepted the possibility of failure as a result of an imperfect performance of the ritual, and the people resigned to other worldly rewards for earthly failures. Assuming that the villagers are not "all the people" to be considered in this given case, or that some of these villagers were not reconciled with the consequences that a failure of the snake skin cure would precipitate, we should no longer be able to consider the snakeskin method as "good" under all given circumstances.

Consciously or not, the boy and the school teacher were not reconciled with such possible consequences of a failure. Physical health and physical survival were their criteria. Physical recovery was their *conditio sine qua non*. In other words, they reasoned in terms of our modern society with its emphasis on technological and scientific progress, with hospitals, medicine, doctors, nurses and many laboratory technicians, and with its emphasis on physical welfare as a goal. Their reasoning took into consideration the fears and wishes, hopes and convictions of all the people who are committed to technology and sanitation, all the people who would not think in terms of ritual, magic, mystery and miracle, but in terms of laboratory evidence, statistics and test tubes.

The people thus committed are a very much larger group than the people in the village. To think and act in terms of this larger group, to imply through one's actions that one is aware of their wishes, hopes and deepest convictions, briefly, to imply through one's actions that one gladly accepts them would seem "better" than to think and act in terms of the village only.

But why would it seem "better"? Because the larger group is "right"? Because their faith in technology, science and medicine is borne out by objective evidence? It is not so easy to endorse the argument offered after "Because." If you insist on letting the evidence "speak for itself," you can rely on people only who are already prepared to consider as potentially valid the type of reasoning through which your "scientific" evidence can be expressed. To convince them with a reasonably good chance that they are capable of being convinced, you must make sure that they are accustomed to the techniques of scientific reasoning and that they are willing seriously to consider the arguments of a "scientist." Before being convinced by the force of certain arguments they must have faith that such arguments might be forceful.

So, if a course of action is "good" because it implies an awareness of the very large group of people who are committed to medicine, science and technology, if such action is "better" than an action which considers the villagers only, the reason why one action is "better" than the other cannot be the evidence of the superiority of medicine (science and technology) over magic and primitive customs. The reason why such an action is "better" can only be the fact that it implies a readiness to reason in terms of and thus to *accept* a very much larger group of individuals than the villagers are aware of. It is then "good" and "better" to be aware of "more" people (to consider "more" people as ends); it is "bad" and "worse" to be aware of relatively "few" and "fewer" people.

If some members of the larger group do not feel that their deepest aspirations are taken into consideration by courses of action implicit in modern medicine, science and technology, such people would feel that they are not sufficiently accepted as ends, for their own sake. Any action intended to be "good" for the entire larger group, would not be quite so "good" in view of the fact that some members of this group are not included. Christian Scientists, for instance, could not fit into this larger group happily.

The villagers, on the other hand, if their course of action is considered "bad," can be blamed only for the fact that they did not show any awareness of the existence and convictions of a large contemporary modern society of believers in medicine, science and technology.

We, the observers, might contemplate a course of action "better" even than that of the villagers, the boy and the doctor. We have learned something about psychosomatic disturbances and that the effects of certain disease carriers

are determined also by the patient's psychological frame of
mind. Let us assume that, along with the doctor and the
nurse, there had come a clever psychologist. In simple terms
this person might have explained to the villagers the concepts of infections, disinfectants and injections. He might
have known better than to reject flatly the snake skin
method. Diplomatically, he might have suggested that the
emergency did not allow for time spent on properly performed incantations and ritual applications of snake skins.
Thus, the villagers might have become more amenable to
permitting a substitute emergency treatment. Given the assurance that their old ways would not be held in disrepute,
in other words, treated as people whose aspirations are
considered, the villagers made ends, not means, might have
become less impervious to the new methods.

Such an approach might seem "better." Why? Because it
would have been indicative of an awareness of "many more"
people. In addition to the group of villagers and to the very
much larger group of modern, science-minded contemporaries, there would have been the awareness of the existence
of psychotherapeutically experienced cultural anthropolo-
gists, and of all such people as are concerned with the intro-
duction of progressive ways of living to superstitious primitive peoples.

Chapter XXVI

TWO FOCI

THE experiences of an individual, be they ever so personal, can be taken as signals that there are other individuals. His actions are "good" and "better" as he, through these actions, implies that he is ready to accept the fact of the existence of others. In other words, his actions are "good" as they imply others, more and even more others. His actions imply the awareness of the aspirations of others, awareness of how life looks from the point of view of others and even more his awareness of others as ends. Any given moment in the life of an individual might become somebody's opportunity of being noticed for his own sake, as an end. But for that moment of awareness and glad acceptance offered by the former, the latter might never be noticed for his own sake, as an end. The individual *acts* at any such moment when he manages to look at life from the point of view of another individual. This is the first focus.

There is the second focus, markedly opposite, the "eternal" moment. In this second context, any given moment in an individual's life might become relevant whenever and wherever he experiences a new occasion to reactivate the relevance of that "earlier" moment. That "earlier" moment being (E), the later moment being (NE), the former and the latter neither are successive nor simultaneous; they are not located on the line of time. The world's full measures of challenging experiences would not suffice to explain the relevances of the "earlier" moment.

The individual is a self effacing creature as he is a signal signifying at any given moment the existence of others, his experiences then being means (pointers), the other (those pointed out) being ends. The individual is a self enhancing creature as his experience at any given moment of his life is a timeless end.

CHAPTER XXVII

BETTER START WITH ONE!

IN some instances there can be a misunderstanding about the meaning of the "larger number of people" in relation with "good" actions. Preferably one might speak of "relatively larger" and of "relatively smaller" groups.

It is a paradox that a concern for a "relatively larger" group, the "better" concern, can be shown more easily by being interested in one person. This "better" concern can not be shown so easily if one begins by being interested in groups of people.

To be thoroughly interested in one person, to love this person in a fatherly or motherly way, or as a friend, or lover, is to accept this person unconditionally. It means that one is interested in many aspects of a personality, in "more" and "more" aspects, in "relatively more" aspects, and, then in ever so many "more." Now there is an element of choice in our way of defining a personality aspect. We may see kindness in a person, or just kindness to animals, or, possibly, kindness to clean domesticated animals, or, maybe, kindness to dogs only. A personality trait may be applied to a limited sphere of performances or to a wider sphere. Ever so arbitrarily defined, however, any personality trait implies the fact that we are aware of people who have something in common, namely a certain trait. The very use of the phrase "kindness to animals" implies that somebody will visualize the meaning of the phrase and understand. A beloved trait in a beloved person would be appreciated more vividly if one only were able to realize what such a trait (as, e.g. "kindness to animals") actually does mean to many people. Now to realize what such a trait really means to people, is this not a method of becoming aware of the very existence of these people, ends for us, not means, inasmuch as we become aware of what is really important to them, not only to us? The effect would be mutual: the more all those friends of animals would mean to us, the more would we be qualified really to appreciate this trait in the character of our single friend, his "kindness to animals."

But we do not stop at the discovery of one trait. We define more traits than one in a beloved person. To be really excited about each one of the many discovered traits, each trait must be noticed with a full appreciation for what this trait does and could mean to people. So again, "more" and "more" people are viewed as ends, with reference to what is really important to them, "more" people than when we were concerned with one trait only, "many more," "relatively more" than when we started to love our single friend's "kindness to animals."

Progress in learning how to love one person, is progress in learning how to love mankind. Or, as Hölderlin expressed it: "Our hearts cannot sustain the love for humanity if there are no human beings whom it loves."

It does not work the other way though. A love for mankind is no certain indication that there is love for one person, that one person will be loved. Don't plan even to start by loving one group, ever so large. By starting with a group, we would have to specify how large a group. The answer would have to be a number. No such number can be given. The difficulty lies in the definition of personality traits. An appreciated, beloved trait in one person is rather arbitrarily defined. Rather than to define "kindness to animals," we might define "kindness to dogs provided that they are almost completely housebroken." Voluntarily defined, the traits will be as "many" or as "few" as we manage to distinguish. Our idiosyncrasies may govern our definitions and distinctions. Now dealing with a group, we would have to define the *differentia specifica* applicable to all members of that group. Letting first come first, we first of all would have to check up on each member, ascertain whether or not he shows the differentiating trait which would make him a member of that group. Love would have to be put aside while we are busy checking. In the process of checking a mistake could be spotted. Somebody might turn up as not eligible. He would have to be discarded. This may happen more than once. Still no time for love. If we have to drop too many, we might find it advisable to redefine our *differentia specifica*, make group membership more flexible. After such "rethinking," there is bound to be "rechecking." No good prospect for loving.

CHAPTER XXVIII

NO POPULARITY CONTEST

THERE are people who are socially conscious of many other people. Their aim in life is a kind of sociability and popularity. This is often confused with the concept of "awareness that people exist as ends." Those popularity seekers do not start with a genuine interest in one person. They start with a group, preferably a very large group. For instance, they want to be well enough acquainted with all the people whom they might wish to invite to their homes, or by whom they might wish to be invited. So they start with this group, not with one person only. Everybody's friend, the "most eligible young bachelor" or many a tea-pouring dowager, surely wants to "meet" people, is "so glad to meet" them, and is noticeably impressed with anyone one ought to know. Surely they are anxious to be aware of as many as possible. The trouble is that they are not aware of enough people. They look at the group from one point of view only: will the people of that group be worth meeting so as to serve as a means for social (and, possibly, material) promotion? If they were left to their own devices, motivated only by social successes, the popularity seekers would not be interested in anyone but socially successful persons. As for them, people other than the socially prominent need not exist, and socially, such social lions interest them only inasmuch as they are social promoters and surely not because of any other trait of their personalities. The popularity seekers would look at people only as if those people were illustrations, allegories signifying one meaning: competence as social promoters. Now there is no such person who is only a social promoter. No matter who he is he must have other traits, traits that could be appreciated more adequately. So if you start with a group, you are likely to make one trait (or a few traits) the property which justifies you to consider the group as a category. You are less likely to notice other traits which do not appear to be related to the category. This is not the way to become keenly aware even of one person as an end. If you start with one person and with one trait of this person, and then another trait and another, and regardless of whether or not this person will ever seem to fall into one category, you eventually will become keenly aware of this one person, of his many traits, and of all the people to whom each one of these traits is really important.

But we were speaking of experience as if they were in time, on a line of time. We also might think of experiences as relevances, not located at any one point on the line of time. In that case, too, the popularity seeker who is bent exclusively on social success, would seem to make a mistake. To be lived as "timeless," an experience must be made relevant. New situations (NE) must be set off against background situations (E). The relevance of (E) to (NE) will be more vividly experienced if and when the (NE) is rather markedly different from the (E). If (NE1) looks very much like any (NE2), there is no vivid feeling that (E) can be made relevant to a wide range of widely different (NE's), and thus become "time less." If (NE1) is a new acquaintance, not very different from (NE2), another new acquaintance who belongs to the fraternity of (NE1), (NE1) is remarkable only as another fraternity member. Old feelings involved in making new friends, will be relevant to (NE1) and to (NE2), but (NE1) is almost like (NE2). How uninteresting! Obviously, the popularity seeking fraternity brother welcomes only one type of (NEs), namely, fraternity members. The relevance of past experiences (E), cannot impress him. Neither can a wide range of (NE's) really challenge his (Es). So he blurs his feeling for the "time-lessness" of the relevances of his (E). So he does not escape the ephemeral.

Chapter XXIX

NO SALESMANSHIP

THERE is another instance where a concern for a large number of people is deceptive. A commercial sponsor on TV, e.g. may claim that he is interested in certain public needs by advertising such merchandises as would help to meet such needs. He too begins with a large group, with as many prospective buyers as possible. He is really interested in one trait only: willingness to buy his article. He is not concerned with traits other than indications that there is a willingness to buy. He has no time to notice other personality traits which might seem irrelevant to the willingness to buy. He also has no time to become aware of the existence of people who might be interested in such traits of other people as would make them unwilling to buy, or indifferent to his wares. Now since there is not one person whose only trait would be his willingness to buy a certain merchandise, the commercial sponsor cannot become aware of one real person, one person who would exist as an end, endowed with many traits utterly or partly irrelevant to the problem of buying.

The harassed sponsor may feel that his sense of business competitiveness is necessary for a healthy economy. He might feel that, all in all, all people with their many individual idiosyncrasies would find it easier to live as they wish to live, if they lived in a competitive economy. There might be struggles, temporarily, but in the long run, all would be well in a world of competitive struggles. We are not requesting our sponsor to hold such a view. But if he does hold it and acts in accordance with it, his activities are motivated by a concern for a large number of individuals, ends, not means, people whom he wants to live under such conditions as would be most conducive to their individual needs and wants. This would be "better," "relatively better" than if his actions were not motivated by such concerns. To prove his case, however, the sponsor would have to find at least one person able and happy to live under the conditions defined by the sponsor as the premises for a fully individualized life.

CHAPTER XXX

NOTE FROM THE UNDERGROUND

THE socialist school also make up their blueprints by beginning with a larger group of people, not with one person. If indeed they could, they would begin with the largest possible group—with all people, numerically speaking. They think they have a blueprint which, if carried out in actions, would make everybody as happy as a person ever can and should expect to be. The very suggestion that a person might need something not provided for in the blueprint is tabu. The printers of the blueprint are determined and confident to reach everybody.

They do not succeed. But let us assume that they have reached one person. There is a good chance that this person will desire something which will not be provided for in the blueprint, and that he will wish to occupy a place which is not quite the one assigned to him in the blueprint. If the blueprinters were concerned with this individual as an end, they would have to stop and notice his unorthodox desires, and that there are people to whom this person's unorthodox desires make sense. This is precisely the outlook which the blueprinters would not understand. They want a world of people unreservedly committed to a predetermined blueprint. They want to proceed as if there were no people other than the unreservedly committed. As a result, the blueprinters are aware of very few indeed, of those only who would be completely committed. It is safe to assume that not one is completely committed to a predetermined blueprint. So the blueprinters are not fully aware of one single person.

The socialistic blueprinters are aware that many people

are hungry, badly sheltered, badly clothed. Monsieur Vincent was also aware of this fact in the days of the Three Musketeers. Old and weary, he gently instructed a young country girl who had just arrived to serve as a nurse in one of his poor houses: "You must feed the poor, he said to her, and take care of them. But you must also treat them so that they will forgive you that they depend on you for food and care." Obviously, Monsieur Vincent's conception of human nature allowed for a loophole in his blueprint of social welfare: in addition to food which humanizes the subhuman, he perhaps saw other needs of a human significance. In short, Monsieur Vincent seemed to have been aware of a "relatively larger" number of people: the poor, and all the people who though hungry, are proud and humiliated because of their dependence on charity. A course of action performed in this spirit was "relatively better."

This critique of the socialist blueprint is not ours, but Dostoyevsky's. In 1927, Sakulin, a literary historian, Soviet citizen and academician, wrote a succinct history of Russian Literature, published in German as one of Oskar Walzel's *Handbücher der Literatur Wissenschaft*. Sakulin gave a short analysis of Dostoyevsky's critique of socialism in the *Notes from the Underground*. There is a misfit, a failure, one of the insulted and injured. It is evident that the misfit needs medical attention, sanitary living conditions, and dental care. So the socialist planners propose all those improvements. The proposals are good. But what if the misfit is too slothful to improve his life? Or too recalcitrant? Well, the proposals being good, it stands to reason that the misfit be urged to consider, urged more urgently, compelled if need be, and, if need be, liquidated. The original proposals are not bad in themselves. But what if the misfit did not wish to follow the suggestions? He was an individual. He might have had notions of his own about life and about his own life. These notions might have been taken seriously by people able to appreciate his peculiar, personal inclinations.

CHAPTER XXXI

OUTSTANDING PEOPLE ARE MEANS SO THAT
PEOPLE BE ENDS

THE individual acts inasmuch as he points toward the fact that people other than he exist as ends. The individual acts "relatively better" as he points toward the fact that "relatively more" people exist as ends. To act "better," he concentrates on one person in order to avoid spreading himself thin by concentrating on a great many.

However, in his state of unredeemed despondency, the individual does not want to "waste his time" by concentrating on an unimportant person. He'd rather have somebody "worthwhile," a celebrity.

There is nothing wrong with celebrities, geniuses past and present, outstanding people, Ph.B.K's, valedictorians, tycoons, Leonardo, Galileo, Einstein, Miss Rheingold. If, for the peace of his mind and to assuage his yearnings, the individual has to start with an outstandingly conspicuous person in the limelight of public attention, let him! He might find out that his hero is great inasmuch as this hero has made it easier for us to point at a "relatively large" number of people who are ends. We must have the courage to admit it: a "great" person is "great" inasmuch as even his very personal and seemingly irrelevant experiences can be read, *with relative ease,* as pointers toward the fact that a very large number of people exist, as ends. Usually it is taken for granted that there is first a "great" person, and, secondly, a large number of people indebted to him for certain benefits and achievements. It is possible to come to such conclusions. But it is also possible to reach other conclusions if you carefully examine the situation in another way. There is a person, past or present, whose very personal experiences can be read, *with relative ease,* as pointers toward many people. This relative ease is the index for the "greatness" of this person. "Greatness" in human achievements thus becomes a means, a means for us to facilitate the process of becoming aware that people are ends. In this way of thinking, "great" people are ends not because they are "great" or important but because they make it so obvious that people are important.

CHAPTER XXXII

PRESIDENT MASARYK, OUTSTANDING—
SO THAT PEOPLE BE ENDS

THE late President Masaryk, founder of the Czech Republic
after the First World War, is considered a "great" man, so
much so that the present Iron Curtain government in Prague
has deemed fit to revile him at some expenditure of TV time
and energy. Yet he was such a "great" man that even one
of his casually remembered boyhood experiences easily can
be read as evidence for the existence of many people, ends,
not means.

A horse drawn carriage impetuously raced down a street
in Brno. A baby was lying in the midst of the street. The
crowd on the sidewalks rushed to and fro, screaming. The
child seemed lost. The carriage thundered along. But the
child was unharmed.

Today we know who Masaryk eventually became, an
ardent Czech patriot. His life's energies were devoted to
wrench the independence of the Czechs from Austrian Haps-
burg domination. For many years the task seemed impossible. Yet Masaryk never despaired. All his life he kept looking for an opportunity to establish Czech independence.
Even though common sense told him often enough that hope
was slim, he kept his faith that an occasion was bound to
come about. There came World War One. There came Wood-
row Wilson with his Fourteen Points and with the principle
of self determination (*Selbstbestimmungs-recht*). There was
the opportunity. As if by a miracle, Masaryk lived to be the
revered first president of an independent country.

Masaryk had done "great" things. With "blood, sweat

and tears," with intelligence and ruthless cunning, and in the spirit of undauntedly devoted, sacrificial leadership, he had freed his country. Surely, this memory of his we related is not to be listed among his "great" achievements. Surely not. But the point is that his achievements are so "great" that we can read even this memory as evidence easily produced that there are many people. Thanks to his "greatness" the unconscious selection and arrangement of experiences reflected in this memory, can now be easily recognized in its relevance to many people. Thanks to his "greatness," we now understand that the memory has a message for many despondent people, telling them that, with all the odds cruelly against you, salvation is possible for the pure of heart. An inconspicuous person, not a celebrity, might have had a similar memory, similarly relevant to many people. But only the "greatness" of Masaryk's achievements and fame makes it so easy to discover the relevance of his memory to many people within the framework of his heroic endeavors.

Later on, as a student at the university in hated Vienna, the young Masaryk was infatuated with a Czech girl, a patriot herself, whose brother chose to borrow money from his sister's admirer. Offering an unsolicited reward for Masaryk's helpfulness, this brother also deemed fit to provide the occasion for a tryst. Masaryk was offended, and discontinued the courtship.

This incident is one of old Masaryk's memories as he related them to his biographer, the Czech poet Capek. At first sight, this vignette does not look like the Brno story. But the principle of selection and organization is the same. There is not a Czech baby, but a young woman, in the midst of dangers, in Vienna, in an atmosphere wrought with hostility against the Czechs. She is prostituted by her own Czech flesh and blood (just as the screaming onlookers on the sidewalk had "abandoned" the baby in the street). And there is a racing carriage thundering along—an impetuous lover. How could shame, "disaster" be avoided? Well, amazing as it might seem, miraculously again, there was no shame, there was no "disaster." The words of the myth are different, the ritual is the same. Masaryk again proclaimed his faith in the people of his country. Deeply in his heart he felt that his purity of heart would perform the miracle of salvation. Knowing what Masaryk achieved, we easily see the relevance of this memory for many people, for all the people who would receive the consolation of his message: With all the odds against you, in the grip of passion, and desires, and with some of your brothers against you as they themselves are corrupted corrupters, prove it that in the purity of your own heart, you can perform the miracle of salvation! Masaryk's greatness consists in that he makes it so easy for us to see the relevance even of his personal memories to many people—ends, not means.

CHAPTER XXXIII

HELEN KELLER OUTSTANDING—SO THAT PEOPLE BE ENDS

IN her autobiography, Helen Keller remembers the roses in her garden in the South:

> But the roses—they were loveliest of all. They used to hang in long festoons from our porch, filling the whole air with their fragrance, untainted by any earthly smell; and in the early morning, washed in the dew, they felt so soft, so pure. I could not help wondering if they did not resemble the asphodels of God's garden.

This memory reads like a myth, with the stage properties necessary for the performance of a glorious ritual. The ritual is Helen Keller's life, a heroic struggle against powers of darkness, blindness and deafness, and a victory, a proof triumphant that one can be sensitively committed to a world which one can neither see nor hear. Life is so much more than one can see or hear: the fragrance of roses and the touch of roses. Life is so much more than anybody could ever see or hear: a hierarchy of values, the spiritual, the unseen, unheard, superseding the material. Beauty is beautiful as it resembles the beauty of God's garden accessible only to the searching soul. It is easy to see the relevance of this memory to many people. But it is Helen Keller's greatness which has made it so easy for us to see the relevance of one of her personal memories to many people.

CHAPTER XXXIV

EDUCATION: THE INDIVIDUAL OUTSTANDING— SO THAT PEOPLE BE ENDS

AN individual is "great" to the extent to which he makes it relatively easy for us to discern the relevance of his experiences to a "relatively large" number of people. A person is "great" because, through him "relatively more" people are treated as ends. Through him, it becomes easy to treat them as ends.

We are, then in a position to suggest a tentative definition for the education of individuals: this education is a way of making people "greater." *An individual may be called educated inasmuch as it is relatively easy to ascertain his relevance for "relatively more" people.*

Now to be "great" and on a high level of distinction, a person must have exerted himself. Yet an ordinary person, not capable to exert himself in strenuous efforts might be surrounded by people imaginative enough to see his relevance to many people, imaginative also to make us see the relevance to many people of that ordinary person. If such is the case, even an ordinary person might become "great."

These suggestions concerning the meaning of education are not a new theme extraneous to this essay. They are implied in our treatment of what we have called the first and the second problem of the individual; his relationship to the world of others and his equality with others. An individual is related to others as we, his observers, are resourceful enough to see his relevance to others. The educational implication now is: the individual is educated, relevant, important, as he has made it easier for us, to see his relevance for "relatively more" other people. Through his very existence, as an end that is, and as a result of whatever his efforts have been, the educated individual makes it easier for us to discern that "relatively more" people are important, relevant through their very existence. An individual is equal to others as he constitutes for us as good a motive as anybody else for our interest in "relatively more" people. The educational implication now: the individual is educated, relevant, important, if we have learned to see that he offers as good a motivation as anybody else, for our interest in "relatively more" people.

Related to others, and equal to others, the little girl with her memory of the circus would be educated if, through our conviction of her significance, she made us immediately aware that even her memory of the circus implies the relevance of a "relatively large" number of individuals. Apparently she is not yet educated. She has not yet made it easier for us. She has not yet made us immediately aware of the relevance of her memory of the circus. So we had to exert ourselves on her behalf.

Related to others, and "equal" even to Virgil, the boy from Brooklyn with his memory of having been run over (almost), would be educated if he were able to make us aware more easily that he may inspire us to understand more people. He too does not yet seem educated. He has not yet made it easier for us to see the relevance, even of his memory, to the problem of "equality." So we had to make an effort on his behalf.

CHAPTER XXXV

EDUCATION: THE KITE-FLYING ENGLISHMAN

THERE is the boyhood memory of an Englishman: he loved to fly a kite. Kite-flying was the favorite recreation for himself and for his parents on Sunday afternoons in Hyde Park. In fact, this hobby was the one and only keen interest which kept the family together. The boy met a girl and married her. He did not allow his mother's disapproval to interfere with his marriage. Yet the kite-flying afternoons were disrupted. The young wife (who also was then a daughter-in-law) had no use for kites. Even worse, she did not like it at all to see her husband stealing his way back to his parents on Sunday afternoons. She went so far as to smash her spouse's latest and most ingenious kite model of a kite. He protested. He beat her up. He was sent to prison. Eventually, however, he left prison and returned to his parents. There, living with his parents and accepted by his mother, was his wife flying a kite.

This young Englishman is hardly a "great" man, nor is he particularly educated. Could he be educated? He could. He could make an effort, learn something, do something, make people aware of accomplishing something. Eventually, he might become a factor in the lives of people. They might notice that he is a factor. In the course of observing him, and without his conscious, deliberate effort to explain the meaning of his highly personal experiences with kites, people might find it easier to understand a meaning of his experiences. Quite unintentionally, his experiences assert that there are many people who must be accepted as ends, the way they are at a given moment, not the way they should be or better be. There are many people living a simple life among simple people, living to keep alive, yet still managing to live with some zest. Their wings clipped, somehow they never seem to renounce the urge of soaring, people who harbor the illusion of free movement, even though they are grooved into a confining track. The kite flier reminds us that there are such people, for better or worse, and that we must learn to think in terms of such people.

Quite involuntarily, if he were educated, the kite flier would make it easier for us to see that his experiences point at "many more" people, people who wonder whether or not such a kite is merely a toy or still somehow the subconsciously lurking symbol of a bird, the external soul or spirit of his owner. Educated, the kite flier, not through a lecture, but through the very impact of his personality, would make it easier for us to realize why there are primitive people who practice the ritual of kite-flying as a method by which men get in touch with the spirits of the heavens, and by which they defeat the emissaries of the nether world. Educated, the kite flier would make it easier for us to feel that we cannot understand him and do justice to him unless we discover a common denominator in the behavior of people so different as the kite flier of Hyde Park and the anthropologically intriguing celebrants of a ritual of kite-flying. Educated, the kite flier would make it easier for us to realize that to understand him, we must be aware of many people.

CHAPTER XXXVI

EDUCATION: LOVE DEGLAMORIZED

WE have suggested a definition for the education of individuals. There is something about individuals which might make it easier for us to see that their existence implies the existence of others.

But we are not happy with our suggestion. We feel now that we have been committed to it, cornered in the conceptual framework of this essay. We have not said what people can do so as to become educated persons in accordance with our suggested definition.

They can love one another. Perhaps we should have said so at once. But we could not take the risk. We were speaking to people chased by the Four Horsemen. On their flight, how would they listen? The very idea that they might love one another has become so charged with unloving connotations that one does not quite know how to introduce it. One has to defictionize the idea, one has to de-Hollywoodize it. One has to "handle with care." One has to make sure that love, first of all, is a breath of awareness. Awareness that somebody exists, in his own way, not in my way, and that I can be quite sympathetically aware of this person's existence in his way. The whole conception of love must be deflated in order to destroy people's notions concerning it. If they want to be individuals, ends, taken for their own sake, there must be such a thing as to accept people for their own sake. So, in order to prove to themselves that there is such a thing, they must accept somebody else as an end, for his own sake. Just to prove that they can do that. That it can be done. That others can do it for them too. That they too can be taken as ends by others. The entire procedure can be described in a much simpler way: to love one another.

Education is a way of learning how to love one another. The teacher, professional or amateur, would be a person who creates this feeling among people that there is this simpler way of describing the complicated philosophical, psychological and sociological aspects of better human relationships: love one another. The teacher also should make people feel that they can afford to use the simple term. The teacher is well prepared if he knows that he will face people who do not (yet) think that they can afford to use the simple term. If he is a good teacher, he will convince them that the simple term is quite all right. Well taught, the people soon will wonder why they were so reluctant about using the simple term.

Chapter XXXVII

THE PECULIAR POSITION OF THE TEACHER

THE teacher, professional or amateur, must teach the simple thing: love, and call it by its simple name: love. Almost since the beginnings of recorded history, however, the teacher has been in a peculiar position: he is facing pupils, children or adults, who do not expect that the thing they ought to learn is so simple. These pupils whom we used to call the individuals in their bewilderment, always expected that they ought to learn something very complicated. In ancient times it was rhetoric and philosophy they expected, and love seemed too simple. In modern times, they expect to be taught the intricacies of science. Now, more than ever, love seems too simple a thing, too unsophisticated and not practical at all.

This peculiar position of the teacher naturally creates a problem of methodology. Normally, he would start with simple things and simple situations, and, from there, proceed to the more involved and difficult, from the well known to the less well known and to the unknown.

Oddly enough, the teacher has to adopt a method just the reverse of what might seem sensible. He must start with relatively complex situations. For instance, when explaining the relationship of people to each other, he cannot simply say: "They ought to love one another." He must discuss and develop an insight into such relationships from a complicated, psycho-sociological point of view, clarifying the terms the best he can, without so much as a mentioning of love. If he is a good teacher, he will command the interest of his students the best he can under restricting circumstances.

There may come a point, however, when he has made his students so interested in the study of human relationships that they begin to show signs of impatience with the cumbersome terminology. This is the point when the iron is hot. At this point the good teacher might offer the suggestion that the word is love. Acutely conscious of his students' mood, he will not say it melodramatically, not as if he were preaching. He will offer his suggestion as a device of unburdening. Burdened with the heavy weight of a terminology which seems to be getting too ponderous, the students will jump at the opportunity of being unburdened. They might be just then most conducive to accepting the simpler word love, just as a substitute for the demanding words, love dehydrated. Once over the difficulty of admitting the simpler word, the students will find it hard to realize how happy they can be. Free, happily unburdened, they will find out that the simple word expresses everything about human relationships, everything, and ever so much more adequately. So much about the peculiar methodology of teaching in reverse.

In this essay, we too have tried to follow this methodology. After all, we maintained that we had something to teach—to teach individuals how to be ends, not means. We assumed that the individuals addressed here are of the despondent, dissatisfied kind. We did not feel that we could afford to ask them for devotion. We asked: "What can you admit about yourself and your relationship with others? At this given moment? And without the underlying implication that you should improve?" We have not yet told you to improve yourself. It seems that various statements could be admitted, indeed, statements concerning four problems an individual has to face: his relationship with others, his sense of equality, the possibility of an escape from the ephemeral and the meaning of his actions. Now as for this fourth problem, it seemed that, to prove himself an end, and so that the proof would satisfy him, the individual must learn that he knows how to consider others as ends. This is the only way of proving with absolute certainty that there is such a thing as to consider somebody as an end. That this can be done. This was then the moment when we felt the need for a simpler way of expressing the same thought. In simpler terms, then, by loving others, he can hope to know that there is such a thing as love. If there is such a thing he can hope to know how to become lovingly disposed toward himself. And he may hope that others may love him as he loves them. So, in this sense, we have applied the methodology of teaching in the reverse,—realizing that our readers might not be willing to listen if one says: love,—but only if one presents the matter in a much more complicated manner, unlovingly. In the end, introduced as a device of simplification, love, the thing and the word, might pass into its own.

Chapter XXXVIII

LOVE ESCAPES THE EPHEMERAL

Before we made the suggestion that love is a simpler word to express the issues connected with the fourth problem of the individual, we also discussed the third problem, the ephemeral. We discussed it without the use of the word "love." If the word had been introduced at that time, the entire development of our thoughts might have seemed easier. But we were not ready to do so then. Love had to be introduced first when we described the individual in action. He can forget himself so thoroughly that he can feel how all his experiences serve as pointers toward people other than he. This capacity for such complete self effacement is love. Deglamorized, dehydrated, the readiness to think and feel in terms of somebody else, and from the point of view of somebody other than ourselves, is love. Even though we may not be in sympathy with somebody's outlook, we acknowledge the simple fact that his outlook exists. This is another way of saying: we realize that there is such a person with such an outlook. For ever so short a time (in calendar terms) we stop to dwell on that realization. For that time at least, the person in question is an end. And this is love.

Now if the very essence of this person, his peculiarly personal outlook, exists in our awareness, surely this person exists in our awareness. He might continue to exist in our awareness, not necessarily until his death, but not necessarily until his death only. As long as we, or somebody else, are aware of the essence of him, of his thoughts, his feelings, his mode of living, he might and he will continue to exist.

How long will he exist? There is no telling. The inevitable objection: "But this is not he, not his flesh and blood. Only a thought about him might exist after his death, not he himself." This objection can be overruled. If somebody is so fully aware of an individual that he forgets himself in the process of this awareness, which one of the two persons exists more really? The one who is so full of his awareness for the other, that he has forgotten himself? The one whose essence (outlook) actually "fills" the other person's awareness? Do you find it easy to assert that the second exists "less" really than the first?

Quite unafraid to say love, we trust that where there is love, there is an escape from the ephemeral. There is— the terms sounds theological—there is immortality. There is the possibility to immortalize any given moment of a person's life.

At the time when we were not ready to mention love, we elaborately explained that an experience at an "earlier" moment is timeless inasmuch as its relevance may become evident at "later" moments. We now may add that where the experience of a person's "earlier" moment is lovingly remembered, the relevance of this experience becomes evident to our loving concern. There is time for such a moment when an inconspicuous person's experience becomes somebody's loving concern at a much "later" moment. This is equally true for such a moment (around 1200 A.D.) when the redactor of the *Nibelungenlied* wrote up this epic in its extant form. This horridly loveable tale, the content of an "earlier" moment (1200 A.D.), may be raised from the dead through a spellbound reader's loving concern at a "later" moment (1958).

To be lovingly concerned with, say, the childhood memory of an inconspicuous person, means to explore the relevance of this memory for many people. This is difficult. It can be done as somebody cares enough to disclose and to expose this relevance, loves enough to care to teach the glorious relevance of this inconspicuous memory. It is relatively easy to explore the relevance of the *Nibelungenlied* for many people.

Yet who is there to say that "more" love should be expended on the exploration of the *Nibelungenlied?* Who is there to say that "less" love should be expended on the exploration of the memory of one so simple? There is equality in that one is as likely as the other to release the power of love which makes one see the relevance of one as well as of the other for many people. Where there is love, there is no question as to the relationship with people, no question as to equality. There is the life substance of each moment fully alive at any other given moment of love.

CHAPTER XXXIX

KRIEMHILD RAISED THROUGH LOVE

THE *Nibelungenlied* begins with an account of Kriemhild's dream as she tells her mother Ute about it. She saw a glistening hawk followed through the air by two nightly eagles. "This hawk is a noble man," Ute interprets, "may God save and keep him, for he is in danger!" The daughter seems sad. "I shall never marry," she says. "I could never bear the anguish of seeing the tragic end of a noble husband." "What a foolish thing to say!" says the mother.

It turns out that the hawk was a dream image of Siegfried, eventually Kriemhild's dazzling suitor. Two intriguers destined to perpetrate Siegfried's murder, are King Gunther of Worms, Kriemhild's oldest brother, and Hagen, Gunther's devoted kinsman. So the dream is really a preview of an entire part of the epic, up to the death of Siegfried. More than that, the dream foreshadows the entire epic, the events unfolding after the hero's death, Kriemhild's undaunted hostility against Gunther and Hagen, and, in the end, her bloody revenge.

According to Goethe's point of view, the *Nibelungenlied* is as great as the Homeric poems. Let everyone read it, he urged, and let him receive the impact of the poem to the extent of his capacity for comprehension. Let everyone love this poem, we might add. In the earlier portions of this essay when love was not mentioned, we elaborated on the "timeless" relevance at comparable great moments of cultural happenings: the dream of Nausicaa, and the dream of young Joseph in Egypt. We now are bold enough to conjure Kriemhild's situation with the insight of loving sympathy. Filled with sensitivity, we can see her, and feel as she must have felt after the dream. There she was, a young princess, sister of the king. She would expect that her family arrange for a marriage with an outstanding figure in the world of knighthood. Difficulties would have to be anticipated. Whoever he would turn out to be, the prospective suitor, the shining "hawk," the glorious falcon, from the day of his appearance he would fill the court with his radiant presence, and, inevitably, he would dim the lustre of the familiar setting. There would be persons who would feel overshadowed, jealous, envious, especially the two outstanding figures, Gunther and Hagen. A rivalry between the king and his grim kinsman on the one hand, and Kriemhild's suitor on the other, would not be avoided in a society of warriors so susceptible to impaired prestige. Explicitly or implicitly, one way or the other, the king would assert himself as second to none and Hagen would support his liege. Alas, the "hawk" would outshine the eagles, and alas, the eagles would show their true colors.

It all came as was foreshadowed. Kriemhild's dream was a survey of danger spots she expected to encounter. The entire *Nibelungenlied* only tells in full length how it all happened precisely as expected.

The foretold plunge into the world of Kriemhild is a work of love. We forget ourselves, we are all in the realm of her fancy; we see the world as it must look from within her soul. When was Kriemhild "more really" alive? At the moment when the poet told her dream, or, at that "later" moment when the poet's dream tale lives in us? Around 1200? In 1958? Made relevant to us by our work of love, this dream tale lives whenever and wherever somebody like us loves it enough to experience its relevance. As there is love for it, it is immortal.

CHAPTER XL

"WHAT DO YOU MEAN, MY MOTHER?"

KRIEMHILD's dream is famous. The epic is considered one of the world's "greatest." So it is "relatively easy" for us to notice its relevance. In the case of a young junior-high school teacher, it is not so "easy." He too has a story to tell, not a dream, but a memory of his childhood.

He too might benefit from a work of love. His memory might become the object of sensitive intuition. Somebody would have to forget himself for a little while, and be filled with insight into that childhood memory which, then, would live while there is love for it to make it live. This memory too, might be declared relevant to many people. A friend might be moved by love so as to educate many people to have insight into that memory, and that is to say, this friend would have to make it "relatively easier" for many people to notice the relevances of that memory. This friend also might make it "easier" for the junior high school teacher himself to notice the relevance of his own memory. Loved and immortal while it is loved, this content of this memory might seem as relevant as Kriemhild's dream. Or, at least, it would be difficult to show in what sense this memory would be less relevant, or relevant to fewer people than the beginning of the *Nibelungenlied*.

This junior-high school teacher was brought up on the so-called lower East Side in New York City, where many people live a difficult life and where they are a little disinclined to show their need for affection. They are not quite sure that anybody might love them. So they decide to be a little antagonistic. This is not such a bad idea as one might think. If you don't expect a sympathetic response from your fellow men, you yourself might as well start by being hateful. If the response is hateful, you may say to yourself: "I asked for it. Who knows? If I had not been cross, the other fellow might have been nice. But one mustn't take chances!"

Our young junior high school teacher remembers a sentimental old lady who asked him (when he was about five): "Don't you love your mother?" His reply, as he remembers it, was a counter question: "What do you mean do I love my mother? What has she done I should love her?"

There is no real "greatness" in this incident. It is the memory of a person, though, the result of selections and arrangements of bits of experiences as only this individual would have been able to select and to arrange in the autonomous privacy of his very own, unique self. This person might be shown a little interest, a little consideration for the fact that he is this person, at this given moment. A little loving consideration. A little love. Why not? Rather than to call it "interest," "consideration," "awareness of the fact that this individual exists in his peculiarly authentic uniqueness," is it not simpler to call it "love"? It is simpler, and it is adequate. Now for the love of this fellowman it is possible that one might notice the bearing of his memory on many people: The people who are not quite sure that anybody loves them; the people who think that love must be earned, like wages or salaries, by "working" for it, by "doing" something for it; people who think that "working" and "earning" are the only real relationships (even between a mother and her children); people who are so distrustful of other people that they do not answer a question, but ask a counter-question, as if they were fencing; people who feel that they have to appear hard-boiled, so much so as not to show any sentiment, not even with regard to their mothers; people who express their callousness in sloppy language; people who have not learned better; people who do not want to know better; people who do not feel that a more polished phrasing would help them to express more polished feelings.

For the love of this fellowman of ours, for the love of this moment of his life when he told us the memory, we actually might make it "easier" for him and for others, to show the relevance of his memory to many people. In this way, we would make him "greater," we would find it "easier" to set forth the "greatness" of his individuality. We would show him to others, and thus, educate the others for an appreciation of his "greatness."

When we stop to think about the meaning of this trivial memory, the young man who gave us this memory becomes the focus of our attention and he has our love, so we need not worry about wasting our time. Seen within the network of relationships and issues at which he points at the moment of that memory, he hardly seems "less" relevant than Kriemhild. True, as we love her for the anguish of her dream, we need not worry either about wasting our time. She hardly seems "less" relevant than the man who asked: "Why should I love my mother?"

Chapter XLI

LOVE MUST HAVE BEEN TAUGHT

THE individuals for whom we are proposing an education, are peculiar in the sense that any explanation without love seems plausible to them. The peculiar position of the teacher requires him to avoid resorting to love as a factor explaining human motivations. At best, love might be introduced into the discussion indirectly.

One continues to wonder because as soon as love is introduced everyone concedes that love is a total explanation— the only thing that has offered any solution for the fate of mankind.

So while it is awkward and delicate to introduce the concept of love, once love is introduced people accept it as their very own. Love, then, seems so other than natural, and yet, so very much more natural than anything else.

Seeming so other than natural, it may well be expected by many to have come to them, as a stranger, to have come to them as an unexpected gift. The concept of love seems so natural, so much their very own, the heart of creation, that they might even come to believe that all created things were created by love and are its creatures. With our determination to accept love as the simpler word of explaining things, and with due regard for man's diffidences, quite naturally we believe that "the world was made by him and the world knew him not" and that "he came into his own and his own received him not. But as many as received him, to them gave he power to become the sons of God, even to them that believe on his name."

Surely, in a world with love as a primary motive, there

is immortality for the individual as there are people whose love for him is not extinguished at the calendar moment of his death, and there is God who taught all this. That God is immortal would not surprise any one, since it is obvious that even any beloved person exists and continues to exist in the love devoted to him and beyond the calendar date of his obituary. That God is love would not seem surprising to the individual who knows about the one and only way of being an individual, an end. To establish a person as an end, there must be somebody who cares sufficiently for that person. Love established people as ends. That God is not the same as the world, would not be surprising. If there were no difference between God and the world, there would be no need for caution about love in human affairs. Affairs are such that the individual in the world is prepared to listen to complicated, involved, and, preferably, to "scientific" explanations other than love. Love, simple as it is redeeming, seems extrinsic. That love may come to seem the only thing that matters, the most natural thing, intrinsic, not extrinsic, would not appear surprising, once we have had the courage to admit it.

Personal or not so personal, human and then not human, only a principle in the abstract, a personified principle, a word that lives: the specific features which might go into a definition of God, will depend on historical traditions and commitments. But that love matters and that it must have been taught, should not seem surprising. All you need to realize is that there is love, hence no death for one beloved, and, since such realizations are not natural but other than natural, that they must have been given to you against the dictates of your natural diffidence.

Chapter XLII

PERFORMANCE OF MIRACLES

The suggestions concerning the education of individuals must not be viewed as an attempt to advocate "natural" religion or "rational" religion in the spirit of the 18th century. Deism, for instance, was a system of reasoning within which some of the other-than-rational tenets of religion were made acceptable on "rational" grounds. Reason seemed natural. It was hoped that religion would seem "natural." For the 18th century "reasonable" and "natural" meant one and the same thing.

In such an age, one of the rationally required questions would be whether or not God is to be conceived as a cause or as primary cause, as the primary mover.

We are not asking such questions. We do not presume that we can offer a rationalization for God. Although we expect the individual to be quite committed to science and reason, we take him on at a moment when he has become diffident and despondent, caught in a web of rationalizations, and willing, quite willing, to accept the advisability of the use of simpler terms. That's when we suggest such simple terms as "love," "immortality" and "faith in God."

Such terms are not conducive to rationalizations. They are useful, but only after the scientific terms have outlived their usefulness. Miracles, if you please, miracles other-than-rational, other-than natural, love, immortality and faith in God, do not happen because of the successful consummation of a syllogism which authorizes their occurrence. To become self evident realities, miracles must be performed. Performed by the individual at any given moment.

There is no need to decide whether or not love is the

"cause" of things, and whether or not God is the "cause" of things. If you say "cause," you put yourself in the context of philosophy and science. You get involved in distinctions as to the use of the term "cause," and as to the extent of its various uses. Proceeding in this way, you have to be detached, objective and impersonal. But how could you be impersonal about the most personal?

Let us face it! You really do not care to be so impersonal. You are too much weighed down with despair to listen. Why do you ask so loudly, (whispering loudly) whether or not love is a "cause"? Are you trying to make a "cause" out of love in order to remove love out of your life, in order to externalize it, make it operate (as a "cause") somewhere in the universe, reasonably far away from yourself? Are you expecting that love perform a miracle outside yourself? Why? So that you yourself would not have to perform the miracle? You are making a mistake. But never mind! This mistake has been made before.

That's where Alyosha Karamazov made the same mistake. He knew love, but even he knew too little about it. He too expected love to be the performance of a miracle somewhere outside. At a crucial moment, when his brother Dmitri was running wild, coming close to murdering their father, during the fateful night Alyosha should have tried to do something to save his brother. He should have been able to help him somehow. He was the only person to whom his passionate brother might have listened. And what did Alyosha do instead? Mourning over the death of Father Zossima, mourning and also rejoicing because the elder had died as a saint, Alyosha sat and waited for miracles to happen so that Father Zossima's saintliness would become manifest. There was no miracle. To the contrary. The elder's body showed signs of early decomposition, earlier than what the monks considered usual, in excess of nature.

Lovable Alyosha had not learned the lesson Father Zossima had taught him. The lesson was not to wait for miracles of love until they might be performed somewhere outside, but to perform them yourself, inside. This would have been so simple. All Alyosha would have had to do would be to try to watch over his brother Dmitri during that night. This would have been the miracle of love performed, the meaning of the departed elder's lesson. That's where Alyosha Karamazov had not grasped the meaning. That's where he made his mistake.

But not irremediably so. The mistake of one moment soon became the glory of another moment. In fact the moment of the mistake turned into glory. For in the night in which he had betrayed his brother Dmitri, Alyosha had a dream. Father Zossima appeared to him with glad news. His soul was saved. One little onion had saved his soul. A few days before his death, Father Zossima had told his favorite disciple Alyosha about a bad person, who had never given anything to anybody, but for an onion he once gave to a beggar. In Alyosha's understanding, so great and all pervasive was Father Zossima's love for mankind that he was able to love even the hardened sinner with the onion. More than that. Father Zossima was able to look at life from the point of view of that sinner. The saint was so utterly oblivious of himself —of his life's long works of charity, so he began to look around for a symbol of genuine goodness. Not thinking of himself as worthy enough to be such a symbol, he could not think of anything more fitting than that sinner with the onion.

Such being Alyosha's conception of the elder's saintliness, he had this dream, and, through it, created the emotions needed for a grasp of the real nature of love. So, at the very moment of his mistake, failing to perform the miracle of love, Alyosha did perform the miracle. In the intimacy of his dream Alyosha did grasp the meaning of the elder's lesson. For he understood that a truly loving soul would bow to a sinner as his superior in love. Or, at any rate, as his competitor.

Chapter XLIII

THE MIRACLE PERFORMED THROUGH COMPETITION

ALYOSHA KARAMAZOV learned how to perform the miracle of love. More important even, he learned that he had to perform the miracle: love requiring the role of self effacement, humility, the humility that is exalting.

But somehow the lovable youth never got beyond the conviction that humility, even the exalting kind, is performed through a ritual of self debasement. That's the way the elder had taught him: self debasement, the potential sweetness of self debasement. In the elder's world there would have been no place for competition, Competition— this American thing least of all things associated with love, giving, self effacement, humility and the sweetness of atonement.

Well, maybe there is no place for American competition in the world of miracles performed by love. Yet maybe there is.

True to our position in regard to the individual, we cannot afford now to tell him that he must be self effacing and not competitive, as if the two were mutually exclusive. We did not deem fit to preach self effacement to him. We only tried to show him that self effacement in the spirit of love is the logical, natural position an individual would come to adopt. Or, if such a position is not natural, but other-than-natural, that the individual would want to adopt such an other-than-natural position. We now admit competition as a quite possible factor in the motivation of an individual. We admit it because we think that it is basically akin to self effacement, because we believe that it is another face of self effacement in the spirit of love. We admit that competition is an essential requisite for the performance of the miracle of love.

Competitiveness can be exalting, a powerful, spiritual drive. It can be performed, Walt Whitman directed, not to raise oneself at the expense of another's debasement, but to rise so high as to be able to lift one up who thinks he is low.

I will leave all and come and make the hymns of you,
None has understood you, but I understand you,
None has done justice to you, you have not done justice
  to yourself,
None but has found you imperfect, I only find no imper-
  fection in you,
None but would subordinate you, I only am he
Who will never consent to subordinate you,
I only am he who places over you no master beyond what
  waits intrinsically in yourself.

This is exalting. The man who speaks nobly maintains that he competes victoriously with all those who compete as to this ability of appreciating a human being, an individual. What's wrong with it is that there is no suggestion of self effacement. Another thing that's wrong with it is that there is no ruthless insistence on competitiveness.

There could have been the insistence that one is so good at this business of appreciating a human being that one need not wish to lift up a person assumed to be low. One even might try to raise a person who thinks he is exalted already. One even might show such an exalted one that he stands higher than he thinks. Indeed, this would be an even more ruthless brand of competitiveness. Of course, to be able to do that would require self effacement in the spirit of love. This would be the miracle of love performed through ruthless competition.

If education is a process leading toward a goal, the goal somebody is to be educated for, *this, then should be the goal for the education of individuals—the miracle of love performed through ruthless competition.*

An individual, educated to be an individual, an end, no means, would know how to behave in accordance with this goal. Having learned that love is not a sacrifice, but his one and only chance for happiness, he would embark on love with competitive zeal. Any given moment would offer the challenge. He would accept the challenge, just to show how "good" he is. Competitively he would be eager to show that he is so "good" as to exalt those who already are exalted. To understand the extent of their magnitude, the great would need him. If they need him, he would be greater than they. He would "beat them to it." This would be competition. Such victory would fill his heart with gladness.

But it would not be a vicious happiness. Educated as he would be, the victorious individual would realize that, if he is "great," his "greatness" rests in that he can disclose the "greatness" of others. His education consists in his ability to see more easily and to explain more easily the significance of others.

Disclosing, exposing, blissfully promoting the significance of others, he would not envy anybody. How could he? Is their "greatness" not his doing? Are they not prominent inasmuch as he has seen this prominence, and has shown it?

Nor would he be possessive about his "greatness." He would not boast that he has promoted them. How could he? He would know that if he can be "greater" than others by seeing their "greatness," it is only because he is capable of effacing himself so completely as to read all his own experiences as pointers toward others. He would understand by now that all he is proves that there are others. How could he be possessive if he learned self effacement.

And he would not regret any loss in the act of self effacement. He simply would be too competitive to regret anything in the act of self effacement. He would begin to discern that, to be so "great" as to see the "greater greatness" of people, he must consider so many many other people (he must see the relevance of the former to the latter) that, eventually, there is nothing in himself but pointers toward other people. So what is there to lose, and what is there to be regretted in self effacement?

Some people may think they have solved the problem of the First Horseman. They now relate themselves to others. The educated individual would not compete in the sense that he might want to prove that he too has solved that problem, possibly better than they. He would use his competitiveness as a prerequisite to perform the miracle of love. He would insist, easily, palpably disclose, that those people have been more successful than they thought they were. This is competition. His endeavor might be challenged at any given moment when somebody would outdo him, showing that these people who thought they were successful, were even more successful than even he, our individual, had thought they were. But there is nothing sinister about such a challenge. Here again, our individual, at any given moment, might outdo the challenger.

Some people may think they have solved the problem of the Second Horseman. They now feel equal to others. The educated individual would not compete in the sense that he questions their equality with him. Ruthlessly competitive in his performance of the miracle of love, however, he would insist and easily demonstrate that those people have been more successful than they thought, "equals" in many more respects than had occurred to them. Again, this endeavor might be challenged at any given moment. Somebody more educated than he, might find an easier way to demonstrate those persons' equality. But so might he, our challenged individual, find an easier way at any given moment.

A young poet, for instance, after the successful publication of his first slender volume of poetry, may feel that he has good reasons to consider himself established as a man of letters, or well on his way toward becoming established.

Recognized, less and less reluctantly, in circles where poetry is being read, he quite justifiedly may feel that he has related himself to poets, critics, lovers of poetry. He also may easily take it for granted that you, unrelated to his world of poets, are not really a serious competitor for him in the business of relating oneself to others. This is your moment of competition in the spirit of love. You now may introduce him to a young girl who works, say, in a printing house. She knows little or nothing about poetry, but she enjoys the patterns of printed lines, the outward, visible form of a poem on a printed page. As far as she is concerned, she produces a poem by assembling letters from a box and making a design out of them. Now, after having been introduced to each other, if they like each other (possibly, even they may be attracted to each other) you may leave them alone. But you also may not leave them alone. Somehow you may help the poet to become aware of a relationship between poetry as a *Gestalt* of meaning and poetry as a pattern of visible signs. His acquaintances in literary circles have not shown him, but you may show him the types of poems set under the direction of poets who thought that the visible setting adds to, and modifies the meaning of poems. You may refer to Mallarmé, for instance. Thus, the poet may come to feel that a concern with the visible setting of a poem, is not irrelevant for a construction of its poetic meaning. Clearly, the girl he met through you—the physical girl with her physical visions, and via the mutual attraction between the two, may eventually make the poet grow as a poet, related not only to his former circles and to the girl, but not only to her either, but through her, to the larger circle of more materialistic people whose chief interests live in the physical world. But as their emphasis on the physical somehow constructs the world of meaning, in ways hitherto unexplored, the poet in his new phase of development, is now related to a much larger circle of individuals: his former poetry circles, the girl, the physically minded, and all those who ask for a less painful union between the physical and the spiritual, and who ask for poets devoted to the creation of poems which would be meaningful not only to poetry circles and not only to printers. Well, if by introducing the young girl to the poet, you have related him more effectively than he has related himself, how are you not a serious competitor in the business of relating oneself to the world of others?

In the business of relating oneself to others you have competed well with the poet, you can feel very proud of yourself.

You also must be doing a pretty good job as an educator of individuals. For there was a man whose incipient greatness was easily discerned in certain circles. You have made it easier for us to discern his significance to a much wider circle.

Besides, in your competitive endeavors, relating the poet to a much wider circle, you have not moulded him in accordance with your wishes. You have treated him as an end. It happened that because of one of his peculiar inclinations, the meeting you arranged widened the circle of his relevance. There is a performance of the miracle of love through competition. The poet, the individual, is an end; there is no way of knowing how many people and how many efforts would be needed to fathom the reasons why this meeting was meant to widen the circle of his relevance.

There is a doctor of medicine, a specialist in the field of pediatrics. He has a considerable sense of devotion to children entrusted to his care. But, naturally, having worked so hard to occupy an important position in medicine, he also has his share of professional ambitions. He claims to be equal in competence to other pediatricians. You, being no pediatrician, not even an M.D., might easily be written off by him; surely you would seem equal to him in many respects, but certainly not in pediatrics. This is your moment of competition in the spirit of love. You now have the opportunity to convince this pediatrician that he is an equal not only to his colleagues in the medical profession, but in other respects, where he hitherto has never considered himself an equal. Let us assume that he is very nice to his little patients. He almost would have to be. But, of course, he has an advantage there. Children are often well trained and more often coaxed, to cooperate with the doctor. If he manages not to hurt them, or not more than absolutely necessary, many children are likely to be quite grateful and responsive. They have learned more or less that one must do what the doctor says. Doctor's orders are even obeyed by dads who don't obey orders. Now the doctor may have to handle a child, otherwise quite spiteful and spoiled, but somehow trained to mind a doctor. In his playful but gently firm association with such a child, the doctor may give the child a new impression of what life is like: perhaps, life is a place where it is not always humiliating to obey somebody who means well.

Thus the doctor who had been a source of comfort in matters of good health, now also has become a source of inspiration in a new area: listening occasionally without resentment, obeying others once in a while without feeling that one's ego is impaired. The doctor might have considered himself an equal only to pediatricians. Now you have shown him that he can be an equal to all those who know how to make a child happy even under trying conditions. To clinch the matter, this doctor's peculiarly unique rough doctor's ways ("rough" by comparison with a doting lady pamperer), possibly Mr. Belvedere's ways, might be this child's unique chance for a feeling of security and childlike happiness. Having convinced the doctor, you surely have become a serious competitor in the business of being an equal. You yourself must be quite well versed in the business of being an equal.

In all fairness, the doctor also would have to recognize you as a good educator of individuals. He was a man whose relevance to a certain circle (pediatricians) was easily discerned. In that sense he was a "great" man before you ever met him. But now you have helped him to discern his relevance to a larger circle (pediatricians, young patients, but also difficult children who need to revise their notions concerning discipline, and their worried parents). So you have made it easier to discern the doctor's relevance in an area where this successful man himself would not have discerned it so easily.

Some people may think they have solved the problem of the Third Horseman. They now manage to escape the ephemeral at certain given, enlightened moments. The educated individual would not compete in the sense that he might want to prove that he too had solved that problem, possibly in a better way. He would use his competitiveness as a prerequisite to perform the miracle of love. He would insist and palpably disclose, that those people have been more successful than they thought they were. This endeavor of his might be challenged at any given moment when somebody would outdo him, showing that these people who thought they were successful, were even more successful than even he, our individual, had thought they were. But there is no pain in such a challenge. He again, our individual, at any given moment, might outdo the challenger.

On her tenth wedding anniversary, a young woman looks at an album of photographs. She had started to keep the album ten years ago. It contains pictures of her wedding, but also photographs taken in earlier years. Her marriage has not been a failure. But it has not been what she would have considered a complete success. Her children are not exactly a disappointment, but would they fulfill the mother's fondest hopes? As she musingly relives many a moment, lost in memories and filled with moods, she is quite an authority in living the timeless moment. She would not think of you as a serious competitor in the business of escaping the ephemeral. This is your moment of competition, however. Now you may show her that she could be a much greater authority.

You may perform the miracle. It's simple. Just ask her if she remembers an incident which is not captured in any of the pictures of her album. She will remember such an incident. Her recollection, though not involuntary (as she has been prompted) will take the shape she decides upon; it will be her selection and her arrangement. Maybe she remembers that moment when, shortly after graduation from high-school, she enrolled for evening classes in a college. Her goal was a career, independence, achievement. One of the college officers at the registration desk talked to a colleague of his. She overheard a bit of the conversation: "It's not only ability, there is also determination." "Oh," said the other, "you mean achievement. Some are overachievers." What was it going to be in her case? Ability? Or overachievement? Over-achievement somehow had a special meaning for her, some-thing like putting everything one has got into verified, certi-fied, lonely records, into drawers, in a fairly well furnished apartment, but without a husband and without children. She went through with her registration. She did reasonably well in her courses, but she dropped out after one semester for fear of overachievement. Now in the light of her album-leafing experience as a wife and mother, she still had not decided whether or not married life was an achievement. Surely it was not an overachievement. But was her married life an underachievement? No decision. But the lack of deci-sion was a decision.

You have prompted this young mother to reevaluate her view as to the meaning of achievement. By making her look at her "new" situation (ten years after the wedding) in the light of "older" experiences which she no longer admitted as valid (for they do not appear in her album of memories admitted as "valid"), you have given her an opportunity. She now may live the moment uncharted on the line of time, the moment when the tree of life had not shed its leaves to be raked away, the moment when life's golden tree was still green. She thought she was quite an authority in recapturing things past. But you have shown her that she is a much greater authority. You have proven to be a formidable competitor.

You are also a pretty good educator. This young woman had thought that she had caught all her really "great" moments, whose relevance she was persuaded to cherish. Now you have made it easier for her and for some of us to see the relevance of a forgotten moment. It too has become "great" and relevant, as if through a miracle of love performed by an educator of individuals.

Some people may think they have solved the problem of the Fourth Horseman. They now take courses of action which lead to the establishment of individuals as ends. The educated individual, in competition with such people, would insist and palpably disclose, that they know better than they think they do. This would be a performance of the miracle of love through competition. But he even may go one step further. He may enter into competition with himself, convince himself that he knew better than he thought he did. This too would be a miracle of love performed through competition.

There is a professor of philosophy at a highly reputable university. He not only taught but also believed in living what he called the life of the spirit, philosophy, music, art, poetry. He also believed that he did not want to act like a snob. He wanted to let the humbly equipped partake of his spiritual riches. So, one day, a sailor wrote him a crudely written letter, telling him that he had read one of the professor's articles in a magazine (on one of those Sunday afternoons when he, the sailor, on leave from his base, between beers and a movie, came across the article in the periodicals reading room of the public library). The article dealt with the humble man's life of the spirit. The sailor was so impressed that he felt the professor poetically had written his, the sailor's, biography. So he had to write to the professor. The latter, pleasantly went so far as to invite the sailor to his home (which was located in a nice neighborhood). The two men talked, conversed one might say. The sailor wrote again, several times, from several distant places. Upon his return to the university city, he again went to see the professor. This time they went to a concert. Really, the cultured man imparted some of his culture to one much humbler. He developed an undeveloped mind. He sharpened the profile of a personality. He modelled an individual. In that sense he took a course of action. He acted.

But he knew better. He knew that, in order to perform a miracle of love through competition, he should contribute to the spiritual growth of his friend, and, then, show him that there had been more growth in the sailor than the sailor thought there had been. Frankly, this the professor was not ready to do. So he did something else, still in the spirit of love performed through competition. The professor began to act as a competitor with his own professional self which, at best, remained a bit supercilious. He began to reason with his simpler, lower, more human self:

"As long as I think that, by imparting some of my wisdom, condescendingly, I am shaping an individual, perhaps I am mistaken. Perhaps I do not yet understand what it means to establish an individual as an end. Perhaps I do understand, however. Perhaps I can afford to share my experiences with my young friend, with the understanding that I might grow as an individual in the process, I, not he, even though it hurts a little that it might be I, not he. Philosophy, art, music, poetry, the life of the spirit as I have learned to live it, is life perhaps only insofar as he too calls it life. Perhaps my life of the spirit is really life only inasmuch as it can be lived, not by me only, but by one who appears to me as the incarnation of life in its mysterious naturalness."

True, this was a professor's way of reasoning. The phrasing was subtle, easily distrusted by people who expect a success story. This is not the story of a success. But it is a

story with a strong degree of success in it. Another version
of Father Zossima's story about the sinner saved by an onion.
The story of a man ready to discount whatever he might
have thought he had accomplished, relying on the saving
grace of the least of all possible accomplishments. Thought
of as a saint, surrounded by impatient worshippers eagerly
expectant of glorious manifestations of a mighty sainthood,
Father Zossima in Alyosha's dream, chuckling, rejoicing, re-
ported that one little onion had saved him. Similarly, the
professor competing within his orderly self with the spirit
of smugness, finally remained assured that his life of the
spirit was real life, *life even from within that sailor*. The
sailor had told him so. This was another version of the success story told by Johann Christian Friedrich Hölderlin, the
poet who, in the days of his incipient madness, when he no
longer could be taken seriously by many, but when he still
could be taken seriously by some, wrote a poem of Socrates
and Alkibiades:

Warum hudigest du, heiliger Sokrates,
Diesem Jünglinge stets? Kennest du Grosses nicht?
Warum siehet mit Liebe,
Wie auf Götter, dein Aug auf ihn?
Wer das Tiefste gedacht, liebt das Lebendigste.
Who most deeply has thought loves what is most alive.

In the terms of this essay, the generous friend of the
sailor has gained stature. He has established an individual,
so much so that he felt as if he had been established by
that individual. He gave so obliviously of his riches that he
thought he was given riches. He came to understand the
business of establishing a person as a person. A formidable
competitor, a performer of the miracle of love performed
through competition.

There was a purpose in this final emphasis on competition. An educated individual need not turn his eyes away
in shame when they talk about competition. This had to be
said. For he might well find it difficult at first to dissociate

competition from a kind of jungle slaughter. It need not be so. Educated as an individual, a person might think of competition as life giver, a preserver of life, a rebirth *in perpetuo* of life, an incorruptible prerequisite for the performance of the miracle of love that is life. Related to others, their equal, alive to moments uncharted on the line of time, and prepared to act in the spirit of love, the educated individual competitively experiences his life as a becoming. *A competitor in that he shows other individuals that they are better than they thought they were,* he can be outdone at any given moment by another individual, by a more formidable competitor. This prospect, however, conceals no tragedy. He too can outdo that competitor at any given moment. There is no offense in this possibility either. For there is hope that he, at any such given moment, might show this more formidable competitor how he, the more formidable one, is ever so much more formidable.

We have faith in such a moment and in the individual (now somewhat educated) and in the rituals and the festivals of the eternal moment.